Worth the Time

a Mom's Invaluable Investment in the Spiritual, Emotional, and Physical Well-Being of Her Children

Paushali Lass

WESTBOW
P R E S S®
A DIVISION OF THOMAS NELSON
& ZONDERVAN

WestBow Press books may be ordered through booksellers or by contacting:

WestBow Press
A Division of Thomas Nelson & Zondervan
1663 Liberty Drive
Bloomington, IN 47403
www.westbowpress.com
1 (866) 928-1240

ISBN: 978-1-5127-5034-8 (sc)
ISBN: 978-1-5127-5036-2 (hc)
ISBN: 978-1-5127-5035-5 (e)

Library of Congress Control Number: 2016911595

Print information available on the last page.

WestBow Press rev. date: 8/9/2016

Dedicated to the Lord Jesus

Who has taken me on this fantastic

journey called Motherhood

CONTENTS

ACKNOWLEDGMENTS

I thank the Lord Jesus Christ for giving me the privilege of being a mother. It's not always been a breeze, but He has provided me with all that I have needed in my mothering journey. A couple of years ago, I felt that the Lord was calling me to write down many of the things that I have learned over the past years, as our family gradually grew from two to seven people! Then He brought us to a new country, which provided me the opportunity to write this book. In the entire process from beginning to the end of this project, there are several people I would like to thank, without whose help and support, this book would not have become a reality.

To Mark, on whose shoulders the kids and I ride—I am so privileged to have you as my lifelong friend. Thank you for being a support for me at all times. Thank you for carrying the load of our family and always encouraging me in my role as a mother. Without your affirmative words, walking through the journey of motherhood would have been a lot harder.

Thank you Joy and Heather, for being my faithful friends and praying for this book. Joy, without your encouragement and "push" I would quite likely not even have got started! I am super thankful to God for giving me such wonderful friends in a new country who have been with me through my ups and downs.

To Istianah, your help and constant good attitude while taking care of my little one has helped me to bring this book to completion. I am so thankful to my God for bringing you to live under our roof and to take care of my youngest, so I could have some concentrated moments of writing.

I would like to extend a special word of thanks for Carey Bailey and Britta Lafont, my coach and editor respectively. I am so grateful for you ladies—for guiding my thoughts, refining my words and for making this book readable. Thank you Britta for taking on this project despite all the craziness going on in your life at this moment with the upcoming move.

And last, but certainly not the least, I would like to salute all the moms in my life who have inspired me to be a wholehearted mom myself. To those moms who perhaps never saw their own worth and the great task they did in raising their children sacrificially, your reward is with the Lord. Ma, even if you think your life has been meaningless, I thank you for your unending love for me. I am where I am today because of you. And thank you to my dear mother-in-law, Mum; I love you and thank you for investing your life in raising your sons and always praying for them. I am enjoying the fruit of your work and prayer today by having a spiritual leader in our home who loves the Lord and is an amazing godly father and man.

INTRODUCTION

Children are a gift from the LORD;
they are a reward from him.
— *Psalm 127:3, NLT*

Thank you for picking up this book. I don't know why you've decided to read it, but I'm happy that you did. Perhaps a friend told you about it and, even though you're not very interested in knowing more about this subject, you did your friend a favor. Or maybe you found the topic interesting because it's something God has laid on your own heart for some time. You might be in the process of wondering how you can have more time with your kids, while juggling the tasks of managing a household and working outside the home. Well, whatever your motivation is, I hope you'll find this an interesting read with something new to learn. More importantly, if you are a mother of young kids—I wrote this book specifically for moms of kids, from infants to ten years of age—I pray that God will use the message of this book to touch you and speak to you personally concerning your own motherhood journey.

I've written all the pages you read here after praying for a couple of years. This isn't something I thought of just the other day while showering! It's been a challenging process with several doubts and ups and downs, as my husband and some close friends can attest to. I was never really a "children's person" before I became a Christian. Home and children were certainly not at the top of my wish list. However, as I got to know God more and more, I had a changed heart and attitude towards my role as a woman, and it's God who gave me new desires.

Ever since I became a mother, I thought that "being there" for my child was the most important thing I could do. However, it was only after the birth of my third child that I felt God touch my heart in a different way, giving me a message and a ministry of *investing* in the lives of my children wholeheartedly, so that they would grow spiritually, emotionally and physically healthy and strong. When I Googled the topic "investing in children," I was a bit surprised. All the top searches concerning investment in children were about financial investment or investing in their education to secure their future. While those things are very important, I was surprised to find hardly any result about **time** as an investment in their growth.

There's a lot of debate in today's world about whether a mother should stay at home with her young children or go out to work. Hardly a day goes by when I don't encounter some sort of opinion about whether it is good for today's modern woman, or her family, for her to stay at home to raise her children. We hear about it from the media, politicians, working moms, stay-at-home moms, dads, uncles, aunts, grandmas… You get the point! Everyone has an opinion to share. Mothers today, perhaps more than ever, are confronted with a barrage of opinions and options about childcare and their roles as mothers. The result? Increased pressure, stress, lack of self-worth, and feelings of guilt whether you go to work or stay at home.

Very few mothers feel free to make their own choices. Or, please note carefully, very few feel free to make choices in line with God's will. If we truly cared about God and His will, then others' opinions and lifestyles would not matter to us, right? Yet we are, to a large extent, enslaved to the society and to what it expects us to be. I wonder though, how often we stop to think about whether our little one's needs are met before we venture into becoming all that we think we were created to be! If you are a believer in Jesus Christ and trust Him to be the

Lord and Master of your life, then you are accountable for every gift that has been entrusted in your care—and your children are His gift to you (Psalm 127:3).

The purpose of this book is neither to condone nor condemn the choice a woman makes concerning work. It is to present an understanding of what it means to invest wholeheartedly in the children God has given us. As with any other investment, this takes time! If we mothers made our choices, seeking God's will and opinion, as to working outside the home or being a stay-at-home mom (SAHM), then there would be less feeling of stress and guilt. As an aside, I don't know who actually coined the term, but we SAHMs don't really stay at home all the time, now do we?

My strong belief is that if we sought God's will first, we would have the peace and freedom that comes from obeying Him. The time we are able to give to work, both in and out of home, may be different at different stages of a child's life. Our end goal should be to raise our children responsibly so that they become followers of Jesus Christ and shine His light in this dark world. Hopefully, by living this way, they will also become responsible and respectful human beings.

As you read this book, I pray that God will reveal or clarify your goals for your own children and that you will ask God, daily, to guide you as to how you can invest in them. This book is primarily targeted at moms-to-be and mothers of young children, particularly from infancy to puberty. Teenage time is a completely different ball game. However, the investment made in the early parenting years can help with parenting during the more mentally challenging and stubborn teen years.

What Do I Mean by "Investing In Children"? I often see advertisements in magazines for workshops on parenting children the best way. There are also a variety of books available on this topic, Christian or otherwise, that get recommended or passed around between moms. Yet, it seems that today's parents want to be good parents in the most convenient of ways. We want easy formulas and quick answers. Books with titles like "Potty Train Your Child in Three Days" or "How to Have an Obedient Child in One Week" are bound to be instant bestsellers. We want results, so we bring home our management goals from work, and we expect to see the desired outcomes within a specific amount of time. Sadly, these methods can hardly work with parenting. We are neither raising robots nor are we running a structured company. We are in the business of raising human beings. And that takes time!

As mothers, there is no substitute for spending time with our children, for getting to know them. Raising another person takes patience, perseverance and, of course, tons of help from God! This book deals with the necessity of spending time with our children. Investing in our kids must be understood to be an *investment of time*. This investment should enhance overall well-being in the areas of spiritual, emotional and physical development. But, I'm not going to be prescribing formulas here such as the number of hours per day we need to spend with our children. What I will give are principles that can be applied to each individual situation.

Let me describe each of these principles in a bit more detail, so you'll know what to expect throughout the the book:

Spiritual Well-Being

As a Christian mama, my heart's greatest desire is to see my kids follow the Lord. I would like them to grow up knowing God and His ways and obeying His timeless truths. This, I believe, is very much our parenting responsibility and should not be left to good Sunday school teachers, books, or Christian DVDs. Moreover, spiritual growth has a direct influence on character formation. A child that grows up in the knowledge of God's Word, and is trained to obey it, will bear fruit in his character traits as well. So, how do we invest in our kids' spiritual growth? Chapter Two and Three will tackle this topic.

Emotional Well-Being

I am guessing no mother would want her child to be sad and insecure. I am also guessing that you, as a mom, want your child to grow up knowing she is loved, accepted and valued. This may even be the reason you're reading this book! How do we raise children who are secure in their parents' love and know that they are loved and accepted by God, just as they are? Please read Chapter Four to get some insight on this topic.

Physical Well-Being

Mothers are nurturers. And this responsibility begins in the womb. Nurturing a child's physical needs is as important in the early years as anything else! Ensuring kids are fed, clothed, washed and kept healthy are very important aspects of investing in our children and must not be overlooked. In Chapter Five, I talk about various things that contribute to the child's physical well-being including healthy eating, the importance of physical exercise, and good sleeping habits among others.

But, first things first. We start this book by looking at the foremost thing that should guide our investment and actions. If we want to ensure our children's overall well-being, we must invest in our own relationship with the Lord. If we are not growing spiritually, how can we train our kids to be spiritual? Also, if we are not secure in our relationship with God and know who we are in His eyes, how can we pass this security onto our children? Therefore, even before tackling the topic of how to invest in our children, we must begin with how we can grow our spiritual muscles, becoming strong in our relationship with the Lord. There is also something else that I will talk about towards the end of this book.

Many mothers often forget to care for themselves because looking after their home and kids is hard enough. After a day of feeding, grocery shopping, cooking, helping with homework, driving around, cleaning, and laundry is there any time or energy left for caring for ourselves? Yet, unless we recharge our own batteries, we run the risk of running on empty and finding ourselves snappy, irritable, and overtired. How do we care for ourselves so that we can faithfully and joyfully serve those entrusted in our care? In Chapter Six, you will get more insight into this topic.

As you turn to the next pages, my prayer is this: *that God would open the eyes of your heart to know the hope to which He has called you, and His incomparably great power for you because you believe (adapted from Ephesians 1:18,19). I pray that you will know God's strength everyday and carry out your work as a mother with His wisdom and power. May God increase and honor your desire to be a mother who raises her children according to the way of the Lord. Amen.*

CHAPTER 1
INVESTING IN WHAT MATTERS MOST

Everyone who competes in the games goes into strict training. They do it to get a crown that will not last, but we do it to get a crown that will last forever.
— *1 Corinthians 9:25*

Have you ever participated in a competitive sport? Or played a musical instrument at a concert? Or simply passed an academic exam with flying colors? If so, you know that none of that would have happened without spending time and effort in training towards that achievement. If we want to do anything well, we must have the discipline to undergo long hours of training. It is the same thing with raising children right. Children are a gift from God and if we want to raise them according to their Creator's ways, then we need to know the Creator first, and listen to His heart on raising His precious creations.

So often, we have a long to-do list and the day goes by without having spent any quiet time with the Lord. We need to spend time listening to Him – through His written Word or through His quiet voice in our hearts. I've had seasons in mothering of young children where I've been so busy feeding, changing diapers, cooking, and driving kids to different activities, that quality quiet time with the Lord has been shoved to the very end of the day. Unfortunately, evening is when tiredness strikes most or a good book or movie distracts me from reading the Bible. And let's not forget that my husband also expects me to spend some time with him then. Where does that leave what matters most? Even as I write it, I realize how ironic and hypocritical this statement really is: If my relationship with God is the most important one, then why put it in last place?

I am very often reminded of this verse: "Where your treasure is, there your heart will be also" (Matthew 6:21). I am so, so, so thankful that God has brought this scripture to my mind often since I became a mother. I acknowledge He is my treasure, yet I struggle to find time with Him. I did realize at some point that it's all about priorities. God is not asking me to neglect very important tasks like feeding my newborn round the clock, playing with building blocks with my two-year-old, cooking healthy meals for the family, or reading the *Very Hungry Caterpillar* for the zillionth time! But He is asking me to set priorities. I need to arrange my life as a mother, within the different seasons of motherhood, to keep God in the very center of it. This means putting God first and organizing the day and its activities around time with God, rather than the other way around! I hope you get the picture. If not, then I will try and make it still clearer.

If I want to flex my spiritual muscles, grow in my knowledge of God, and get closer to Him, then there is no doubt that I need to spend time with Him. You know how new sweethearts want to spend every minute with each other, getting to know each other. When they're not together, they talk on the phone, send one another texts and emails, and exchange Facebook messages. There is a desire, an earnest longing, to know and see each other. I wish for that kind of desire in spending time with my God, too. I am at my best when I actually long to spend time with the Lord. When that kind of longing is there, I wake in the morning thinking about how I can organize my activities so that I can spend my time with God, in prayer and in His Word. If I have young children at home, I plan their nap times so that, while they sleep, I get to spend some of those precious moments with God and a good cup of coffee...or tea if you are British. If I have school-aged children, I look for time in my day to listen to God before running errands, checking homework, or driving the kids to piano lessons.

For me, the best time with God is when I wake early in the morning to listen to His voice in peace and quiet. Unless I am ill or are sleep-deprived from caring for the baby, there is no real reason why I cannot begin my day with God. If you're like me, early morning quiet time can be about praying and seeking His will for the day, and Bible study can be done later if you are not a morning person. It's important to find some time in the day that you can spend reading God's Word, praying and listening to Him without getting distracted, even it is for a short time. And yes, the laundry can wait. The amount of time spent on studying the Word may be depend on whether or not we are caring for a baby or a sick child. There are seasons when we may spend a couple of hours daily, digging deep into the Word. In other seasons, we may not be able to do that. When time is short, I meditate on one verse I've read. Either way, it's important that we let the Holy Spirit of God speak to us and help us to apply His Word in our lives.

I am a mom of five kids and I know that life can be pretty busy most of the time. I have also learned that I can spend time with God doing any household chore—it does not have to be with my Bible, markers, pens and colored pencils out. I can sing. I can pray. I can speak scripture verses aloud. I can meditate on a verse I've read the day before. And I can do all this while I fold the clothes for my family of seven, cook up a fragrant curry, or drive to the grocery store.

Spending time with God and His Word has to do with my desire to be with Him and setting priorities accordingly. If I need to cut down on my social calendar, then so be it. If I have to spend hours in training my little ones to sleep well, so that I can have some uninterrupted time with God, then so be it. If I have to cook that same, simple pasta dish again because it takes less than fifteen minutes, then so be it. Because I know that any time I've gained can be directed towards developing a rich relationship with God. And this is the investment of time that matters most. I'm not implying in any way that you have to copy the way I do things. I have, over the years, found ways to spend time with God that work best for me. I hope you can try and test these methods or find some of your own that will work for you and best fit into your daily schedule.

Motherhood is hard and there's no doubt about that. I know several women who have shied away from parenting simply because they feel it is too hard. Certainly there's nothing glamorous about wiping babies' bottoms and runny noses or having sleepless nights! I've had to sacrifice many "good" things in life in order to raise children diligently. The newborn stage of living sleep-deprived, the 24-hour stints of caring for sick children, the afterschool homework with older kids, and all those minutes spent disciplining and teaching—the time I've invested in my children has left its mark on me. These are the things that have stretched me spiritually, emotionally and physically, pushing me to grow and enriching me. But this richness and fullness happened only because I went to the Lord daily to refuel, recharge, and refill.

Intentional mothering happens only with strength and wisdom from The Source. As we go to the Lord as our source each day, we grow our confidence in taking care of our kids as we learn to do everything by trusting in God, drawing our strength from Him. Let's look at the passage below, reading the words aloud, replacing the word "man" or "one" with "mom" and meditating on the questions that follow: "Blessed is the one (mom) who trusts in the LORD, whose confidence is in him. ~~They~~ (She) will be like a tree planted by the water that sends out its roots by the stream. It does not fear when heat comes; its leaves are always green. It has no worries in a year of drought and never fails to bear fruit" (Jeremiah 17:7-8).

- How can your life, as a mother, be like the tree with deep roots that does not fear and worry come what may?
- What does it mean to bear fruit specifically as a mother? What is the fruit that you are bearing today? What fruit would you like to bear?

My sweet mama friends, I do hope you see the importance of spending time with God first, so that you are able to invest wholeheartedly in your children. If you are currently not satisfied with your quiet times with God, don't fret! It's actually a good to see a need for improvement so it can spur you on to having more intentional time with Him. But ask yourself first: what is hindering me from having time with the Lord? You can start to answer this by writing down all the activities of your day and the time spent on each of them. Are there any activities that can be crossed off your list or time you should spend differently? Use the flowchart below to streamline your activities so you can find more with God and get to know Him better. And one thing I can guarantee you (speaking from own experience) – the more you read God's Word, the more you'll want to know Him. I conclude this chapter with the timeless Word of God:

"Let us throw off everything that hinders and the sin that so easily entangles. And let us run with perseverance the race marked out for us" (Hebrews 12:1).

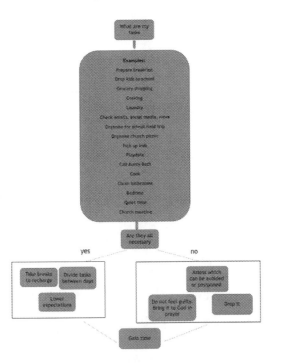

Chart 1.1: Evaluating my Day and How I can Spend Time with God

CHAPTER 2
INVESTING IN THEIR SPIRITUAL GROWTH

*I have no greater joy than to hear that my
children are walking in the truth.*

— 3 John 4

One day, when I am old and very gray, sitting by my fireplace,
and sipping a cup of tea, I hope I can confidently say that I
am overflowing with joy because my children are walking
in the truth of God's Word. However, even when I am not so
old and gray, there is nothing that gives me greater joy than
to know that my children are walking in the truth. I pray they
are making wise choices in the everyday matters of their lives
concerning school, friends, church, family and all the different
things that they are involved in.

Raising children to love the Lord and others and obey
His commands is my biggest desire as a mother. I know that
God is on my side, and He will fulfill that desire as I find my
joy in Him and keep Him first in my life (Psalm 37:4). This is
why we began with talking about how we can maintain and
nurture our own relationship with God first. When we have
our "foundation" in place, we can move to task of "building".

This is the building up of our children, spiritually, so that they will know our God. In this chapter, we will be talking what is important in leading those little people to Jesus. As mentioned before, this extremely important building task does not just happen. Our investment of time, prayer, tears, and effort, and our continually seeking God's wisdom is required.

My children are not teenagers yet, so I am beginning to see glimpses of the fruit that they will bear later in life as well as the fruit that they are already bearing. I have learned my methods by studying Scripture, as well as by getting advice from many wise, older women whose kids are now adults, walking in obedience to the Lord. The following points describe the importance of investing in kids, from a spiritual point of view, so as to raise them to be Christ-followers and responsible people. As you read, pray and to listen to God and take notes on any other points He brings to your mind.

The Importance of Prayer

How much time do you take a day to pray for your children? Five minutes? Twenty minutes? Altogether one hour a day? Does the Bible say something specific about it? The

Bible does say we are to pray on all occasions, and continually (Ephesians 6:18). Praying for our kids is an all-day, anytime, anywhere thing. We can never pray enough for our kids. It's good to cover our precious ones in prayers offered to God, in faith. Praying for your children can start before conception. How many of us have asked God to give us a child? Prayer should continue during pregnancy, the newborn stage, the toddler years and the preschool, elementary and high school years. Our prayers should continue right into adulthood. The prayer of a mother is powerful. I have seen the fruit of prayer of many a mama whose children are now adults. I am personally so thankful to the Lord for my mother-in-law who always prayed for her children, and now I enjoy the fruit of her prayers—a godly man as my husband. I thank the Lord for godly, praying mothers!

Right from the time I was pregnant with my first child, God got me into a habit of praying for the growing baby in my womb. My first pregnancy ended up in a miscarriage. After that tragic incident, I was on my knees every single day, praying for the beating hearts of the healthy babies that eventually grew in my womb. I was thankful to God for every day of a healthy pregnancy, five times after that. Not only did I pray for the safe

11

growth of the baby in the womb, and for a safe delivery, but also that the baby would grow up to know God, love Him, and obey Him. I do believe that God hears the prayers of mothers even before He brings their babies into the light of day. So, if you are a pregnant mama reading this book, then be encouraged to know that God hears your prayers for your growing baby. Pray each day, several times a day. Even if you did not pray for your children in pregnancy, don't worry. God has still got your kids covered. My parents do not know the Lord yet, but the Lord knew me and chose me to belong to Him even before He created me. We know He is faithful and it is never too late to begin praying!!

It's a wonderful privilege to pray, asking the God of the universe to bring your baby safely into the world. Even with amazing medical advancements, many things can go wrong. Not every baby is born healthy. Not every birth smooth sailing. But we can trust God. We can put our anxieties about labor, pain, type of birth-choice, and the post-natal health of the baby and mother—everything—in God's hands, through prayer.

I've enjoyed the privilege of knowing several of my friends began praying the moment I went into labor. This knowledge has always given me peace. Prayer did not take away the excruciating pain of labor, but it did relieve my anxieties about the birth process every time. Then, with the labor of my fifth baby, I experienced the birth in a kind of a miraculous way. It began with a constant conversation with the Lord as to whether to go for an epidural or not. I heard an overwhelming, "No!" Even through the thick of labor, with the anesthesiologist getting ready to insert the epidural needle, I kept talking to the Lord and hearing this, "No!" which seemed quite unbelievable for me. Then, before the epidural was even started and before doctors said my body was "ready" to birth the baby, my little one miraculously came out! The Lord comforted me, and forever touched me, by giving me the amazing experience of hearing from Him through prayer, during childbirth.

As we mothers know, no matter how much advice we receive or how many pregnancy and childbirth books we read, nothing can completely prepare us for the postpartum weeks. We encounter sleepless nights, weak body, embarrassing and unexplained tearful moments, painful breasts, and older kids needing constant attention. It's those difficult moments that provide us with an opportunity to experience God's amazing power and strength in our lives. God's Word can provide us with inspiration and wisdom when we face obstacles. One of the verses that always helped me during the postpartum time says, "But those who hope in the LORD will renew their strength" (Isaiah 40:31).

I'm sure every mother can relate to the anxiety that comes from sleep training. In keeping with Isaiah 40:31, I hoped in the Lord for help in getting my babies to sleep. Every prayer was a desperate cry out to God to help those little wonders sleep, as I could not bear those ear-piercing screams any longer! And amazingly, all my kids started sleeping through the night at about seven or eight weeks. How many sleep training books did I read? One, and I only read half of that with my first child, because I was too tired to read the entire book. Sleep training for my little ones occurred as I came to the babies' Creator, totally desperate and broken, seeking His wisdom on how to let the baby sleep. In the end, my little ones learned as a result of His faithful answer to my pleas.

Apart from the many daily situations that call for prayer—be it concerning sleep, what to feed a fussy eater in the toddler stage, healing of a wound caused by a playground accident, or which preschool to send a three-year-old to—there is something that needs earnest prayer at every stage of a child's life. The most earnest prayer though that we can pray for our children at any age is for his/her spiritual growth. We pray that our children will come to know God through His Son Jesus Christ, to obey Him, and to share His love in this dark world. Let's never tire of praying for salvation and spiritual growth every single day for each of our children.

Praying is not only asking God to take care of our needs and give us wisdom; it is praising Him, confessing our sins to Him, and thanking Him for all His goodness. As we pray, we are modeling the ways our children should worship God in prayer. When they are younger, our prayers are often directed toward physical and emotional well-being. As they grow older, our prayers for our children take on a new dimension as we pray more about their spiritual well-being. We often pray that they make good decisions concerning friends and activities. We want them to read books and watch television and movies, under the guidance and leadership of God the Father. As we spend more time with our kids, getting to know them and the issues that they face, we are able to pray more purposefully for them. Praying for the specific needs of our children is an investment of time and energy that will reap rewards in eternity.

Developing the Habit of Prayer

It's wonderful to see small children depending on the Lord for the various goings-on in their little worlds. Kids can develop their personal practice of prayer very early, learning to praise God, asking Him for help, or seeking His guidance. Children learn to pray as parents, family, or friends model a praying lifestyle. There is no wrong way to pray, but some ways encourage deeper dependence on the Lord. I can set an example by saying the same structured prayer consistently or I can demonstrate how to talk to God in all sorts of situations, saying anything that is in my heart, any time of the day. When I've done the latter, I've seen prayer become a lifestyle for the kids. They've developed a habit of praying to God at any time of the day. In any case, our family prayer life includes both scheduled times of prayer and prayers which dialogue with God throughout the day.

In terms of scheduled prayer time, we pray together first thing in the morning and again in the evening before bed. In the mornings, we thank God for the safe night that He granted us and we seek His protection and guidance for the day that lies ahead. We let the kids use their own words and ways to connect to Jesus. In the evenings, our prayer time includes a Bible lesson. Unfortunately, we've found this time with the Lord can be quite a challenge, particularly at night. There is usually one child who doesn't feel like praying or is so tired that he refuses to listen to a single Bible story. There have been many times when my husband or I have been tempted to forego these precious family worship times in favor of much-needed peace and quiet, but thankfully God has protected us from giving in to that temptation!

As I've mentioned, in our house we have a running dialogue with God, talking to Him throughout our days, praying about any and every thing. In Scripture, Paul calls this praying "continually" (1 Thessalonians 5:17). Our family prays to Jesus every time we started the car engine, especially embarking on a long journey or on an unknown route. One of my children developed the habit of praying whenever we drove in the dark! He would say, "Mama, we need to pray to Jesus and ask Him to protect us, because it's dark!" Once, when our babysitter cancelled suddenly before a very important meeting, another child said very matter-of-factly, "Mama, why do you worry? We just need to pray that God provides us with another help. Let's pray now." I can't tell you how much these moments mean, as a Christian mother, because it shows me these little ones are developing a relationship with their God. Through prayer, they have learned to see God as loving, providing for, and protecting them.

It's easy to teach children to depend on God for protection from dangerous situations or for help with friends or schoolwork. Still, it's our duty to let our children know that God is also a God who judges our thoughts and hearts. Repentance needs to be taught and modeled to our children. Whenever God convicts us of any wrongdoing, or of anything that is not pleasing in His eyes, we ought to repent. Our children must experience coming before God with prayers of repentance, followed by an assurance of forgiveness and restoration. One of my kids has a very sensitive spirit, and it isn't unusual for her to approach my husband or me, in tears, saying how she feels sorry about a certain behavior at school. Most likely in these cases, it is the Spirit of the Lord stirring her heart and we have told her of that. She has learned to go to the Lord in prayer, saying sorry, asking Him for forgiveness and for help to make things right with her friends. Often these moments have occurred just around or after bedtime, just when I have desperately needed some "me" time. Yet, I have never regretted the time I've sacrificed to hear my child's heart, discuss the situation, and pray with her; it has been an investment in her relationship with God and in the development of her personal prayer habits. Seeing such fruit in my young one is a reward from God! These moments are absolutely precious.

There is one important limitation when we pray with and for our kids. What we and our kids ask of God should be in line with biblical teachings (1 John 5:14-15). Of course, we can't expect a three-year-old to pray for everything in line with God's Word, but we must teach them that prayer times are about relationship with Him, not just about asking Him for this and that. Our Lord Jesus has already taught us how to pray. When the disciples asked Him to teach them how to pray (Matthew 6:9-13), He answered their request by teaching them *The Lord's Prayer*, which is a powerful tool that we can use to teach our kids to pray as Jesus did on Earth. We can teach them the principles behind each verse in that prayer and they can use this model to pray similar prayers, in their own words. Teaching kids to pray biblically takes time and effort on our part. Many of us must first learn how to pray biblically ourselves!

The importance of investing in relationship with God and the value of really knowing Him should not be underestimated. As we guide our kids into knowing God, His Word, and His heart, they learn to make wise life choices on their own. Laying this foundation in their early years is so crucial. There is no substitute for reading the Bible with the kids for an all-round spiritual development. From Scripture, kids will see for themselves that God is real, that He listens to us, and He keeps His promises, just as the Bible says. As they grow in the knowledge of God's Word, they'll be more likely to discern what to pray for and how to pray. Children who know God personally move from childish, sweet prayers like, "God, please take care of Mommy and Daddy, and my brothers, and Andy the hamster" to mature and earnest prayers like, "Lord, please show me what You want me to do in life and how I can bring honor to Your name." As mothers, we have a great calling.

We have the power to influence and change societies and it starts within the wall of our homes by simply reading Scripture to our children. The rest we place in God's hands.

Knowing God

For any of us to know God, a miracle has to happen. God has to open our hearts to know Him. We may read the Bible from the beginning to the end and gain a lot of knowledge. However, unless God opens our hearts and we respond to Him, all the knowledge is of no use really. That is why praying for ourselves and our kids or anyone, that we may know God, is so important. God responds to our heart calls. It's a good thing, as mamas, to ask God for wisdom so we can know what to read to our kids, and how to read it, so that they may understand, according to their age and maturity. We get to know our spouses and friends better by spending time with them so we can know what's in their hearts. The same is true for knowing God better. We should spend more time with God and with our children in the presence of God. We must read the Bible with them. It's important that we talk about God, as revealed in the Bible, and teach our kids how He is present in their lives. I find two main family activities that help guide our children to knowing God: reading Scripture and talking about God.

Reading Scripture

"But as for you, continue in what you have learned and have become convinced of, because you know those from whom you learned it, and how from infancy you have known the holy Scriptures, which are able to make you wise for salvation through faith in Christ Jesus" (2 Timothy 3:14-15). Timothy, a man of God to whom Paul writes the above verse, was influenced by the sincere faith of his mother and grandmother (2 Timothy 1:5). How amazing it is to have your name mentioned in the Bible – by simply being the faithful mother who passes on her sincere faith to her son! Timothy was a godly man, mightily used by the Lord to spread the Gospel. Even though the names of Lois and Eunice are mentioned only once in the Bible, we see that their influence was huge. These moms had read the Scriptures to Timothy since he was an infant. This time invested, teaching God's Word, made a big impact on this young man. We see here the importance of mothers in the spiritual development of their children.

Biblically speaking, the mother is the primary teacher under the spiritual leadership of her husband, the father (though, in Timothy's case, his father was a gentile). Teaching at home is not meant to merely supplement the fantastic curriculum taught in Sunday school, kids' church, or AWANA. In a Christian family, time spent reading and talking about the Scriptures at home should be the *primary* source of spiritual development for the children, with other good teaching as an added bonus.

Reading Scriptures can take the form of sharing Bible passages with your baby or toddler while nursing, during other feeding times, or reading Bible stories aloud in a dramatic way so as to captivate their little minds. With school-aged children, Scripture training can involve studying different books of the Bible or going through Sunday school material during the week (and bless the teachers who send homework). Creativity during Bible reading captivates your audience, and this will help them store information about God in their minds and hearts for many years to come!

The next time you think about reading the Scriptures to your little ones as a chore or a tedious, monotonous task—think again! Pray for wisdom. Ask God how to make those Bible reading times interesting for the kids—in a way that they actually *want* to hear God's Word—which will help them lock the truth in their hearts. I am quite sure there will be stages where one or more children in your family will resist or rebel against these Bible reading times. There will be all sorts of interruptions—crying baby, spilled milk, a sudden urge to go to the potty, wriggly toddlers, tiredness—you name it! There will be many diversions to distract us from reading the Bible to our kids. How I wish reading the Bible would always be a peaceful, easy affair!

However, as in any other area of desiring God in our lives, we can expect attacks. Remember, "Your enemy the devil prowls around like a roaring lion looking for someone to devour. Resist him, standing firm in the faith, because you know that the family of believers throughout the world is undergoing the same kind of sufferings" (1 Peter 5:8-9). Even if the temptation to give up on Scripture-reading is high, I encourage you to pray instead, and not to succumb to the attacks of the enemy. No, it is not pleasant to have a pre-teen or younger child constantly refusing to spend time learning about God or His Word. Many moms fear they will be 'pushing' their child away, if he is forced to read the Bible, but it is faith that conquers fear and stands against the enemy's attack.

Don't get me wrong. I am in no way suggesting that your faith is small if your child does not want to know the Bible or go to church, but the way to deal with those situations is through faith in Jesus. As for me, I must often ask God to give me faith because, left on my own, I tend to fear more than trust Him. We must pray, with faith, that God would show us how to guide a disinterested child gently to His Word. Also, it's good to get together with like-minded moms to pray. It's also a great encouragement to come together, intentionally, to share struggles, concerns, moments of victory and tips on improving family devotional time. This kind of support and fellowship can always benefit someone raising young children.

Every family is different, with varying numbers of kids, and unique routines and life-rhythms. What works for my family may not work for yours. However, even as I celebrate the distinctiveness of each family, there are some general guidelines that moms can use to develop a Bible reading/ teaching habit. You may find the following principles helpful for planning Scripture reading time so that it becomes a part of your children's daily lives:

- Teach them: God is almighty. We are to know this about Him and come to Him with fear and reverence (Psalm 33:8,9; Revelation 14: 6,7; 15:4). Therefore, right at the outset, teach kids that this time is holy, set apart from all other distractions, and a time that the family takes seriously.

- Teach them: God is worthy. Begin by worshipping Him with songs, praises and saying specific "thank-you" prayers (Psalm 33:3, 95:2, 100:2). This lets the kids focus on thanking, rather than asking God for things from the beginning.

- Use the Bible. Read a chapter or a few verses from a book of the Bible. You can select a book to read together for a few weeks or pick out short verses from a devotional book.

- Dramatic storytelling works at any age. Here are some options:

  o In your own words, re-tell stories from the Bible with hand gestures, props, or costumes. This makes the Scriptures come alive and feel more real to them, hearing exciting stories from the mouth of someone they know well.

○ Ask children to act out their own favorite stories or passages. This is helpful when the kids are particularly distracted, tired, or less motivated to listen to Bible stories. Suddenly they become animated, as they transform themselves into Noah building his boat or the mockers laughing at Noah. This option works well with children who struggle to sit quietly or are natural actors. It is also fun for the whole family.

○ Discuss how each would child feel, being in the shoes of the Bible characters.

• Show kids how the Bible has answers to their problems. Ask your kids what issues they might be facing in life and then read out a verse that will help them. After all God's Word is to be used as a guide and counsel (Psalm 119:105, Psalm 32:8).

• Take a verse or two to memorize for the day or week. Once again, this depends on age. Children learn so fast and have an amazing memory— it's a pity when their brains are not put to good use! I do believe though, that even as the kids memorize verses, it is our responsibility to talk about those verses and teach them the meaning by asking questions and giving examples from daily life. This way, the memory verse will have more relevance in their lives.

- Keep the sessions age-appropriate.

   o Keep younger siblings occupied: If there are toddlers around in the room, you can think of giving them some picture Bible board books or some attention-capturing toy that will keep them occupied so that you can read Scripture to older kids.

   o Length of time: For younger listeners, those under five years who cannot concentrate for long, five to ten minutes spent with them reading God's Word is probably enough. As kids grow older, allow for more time to discuss what is read. Of course, some days allow for a more engaged Bible reading time than others, but developing the habit of reading the Bible *and praying* is important.

o Reading level: You can read from your own Bible, using simplified words (this does take more effort but is so worth it) or read from a children's Bible. There are several children's Bibles available according to age categories. Until they are three years old, it would make sense to use picture Bibles, moving toward more words as they grow older.

• Do what works for you! Depending on how much time you have, you may choose one—or even a combination of a few—of the ideas above. The main principle here is showing them the importance of coming to God to know Him through His Word.

I hope these principles suggest some options for a family time, set apart and dedicated to the reading of God's Word. Adopting this habit gives an example to the children, allowing them to have focused Bible study and prayer time, just as mom has her "quiet time" with God. This time is necessary and crucial in the spiritual development of a child because the lessons learned from talking about God and His Word throughout the day help children to see God as a person to get to know. This practice demonstrates to them the importance of seeking His truths, wisdom and counsel in their everyday lives.

Talking about God

"Hear, O Israel: The LORD our God, the LORD is one. Love the LORD your God with all your heart and with all your soul and with all your strength. These commandments that I give you today are to be on your hearts. Impress them on your children. Talk about them when you sit at home and when you walk along the road, when you lie down and when you get up. Tie them as symbols on your hands and bind them on your foreheads. Write them on the doorframes of your houses and on your gates" (Deuteronomy 6:4-9).

On a fine crisp sunny fall morning, I went out for a stroll to enjoy the fresh air with my older daughter who was, at the time, all of seven years old. She surprised me by asking whether God had already chosen her, or if He would choose her sometime later, as an answer to mommy's, daddy's, granny's, or grandpa's prayers. "What a deep question," I thought. The next fifteen minutes or so were spent talking to her about some gems revealed in the book of Ephesians about God's election of people. Thankfully, I had read those verses from Ephesians 1 and 2 a few days before, so my memory was still quite fresh. It was such a lovely mother and daughter morning walk, talking about God and His plans! It reminded me of what God told the Israelites when He instructed them to talk about Him and His Word in Deuteronomy 6:4-9. God wants us to make it an all-day, every day activity, even as we walk along the road! I think there's a reason why God wanted His people to think about Him and His Word. Teaching His commandments to our children, through daily application, trains them to think from a biblical perspective or worldview. Growing up in a world that is increasingly devoid of values and morals, it's essential to instill God's Word into the minds of our children as much as possible, whenever possible.

Let me ask you a few questions related to Deuteronomy 6:4-9: Are God's commandments on your heart? How do you impress them on your children's hearts? What are some ways that you intentionally talk about God to your children? What are the areas in your family life that are carried on, without bringing God or His Word into it?

I spend a substantial part of the day driving. There are play dates, shopping trips, doctor visits, school drop off/ pick-ups, sports and cultural activities. All of this time driving around with my kids in the car gives me plenty of time to talk. Of course we do listen to music too, but I love those car conversations, those natural teaching moments. I've had some of the most interesting conversations about what Jesus would think if such and such thing happened. I've had the opportunity to talk about God's commandments concerning hot topics such as marriage, homosexuality, friendships and salvation. And those teaching moments did not come because I prepared a Bible study or a mini-sermon to preach to my kids. No, those moments came rather naturally, as a response to one child sharing that his female preschool teacher had a "girlfriend" or that third-grade Tom wanted to get married to my first-grade daughter.

Conversations about God and what He would think about a certain situation have become quite natural during mealtimes or when we go for a walk with our babies and toddlers. During mealtimes, our school kids talk about their "BFFs" and other classmates and their daily arguments. This also gives us opportunities to talk about applying God's Word to different situations. I often ask my kids if they can think of any verse that speaks to the situation at hand, to see they know how God would want them to react then. Some of my most cherished moments have been those nighttime or sick-child times when I've spent time cuddling with my baby/child and telling her about God's love. It's been a privilege to share stories from the Bible about healing, giving them hope in times of sickness. I have, on several occasions soothed a newborn baby using God's Word found in Zephaniah 3:17, which promises that God will quiet us with His love.

If children have God as a central part of their daily lives because of talking with Him, praying to Him, and just "hanging out" with Him, then the reality of God's presence is close to them even if He is physically unseen. They will learn to see Him as they experience answered prayers, conviction of sin, and peace "which transcends all understanding" (Philippians 4:7). It's a really good habit to begin the day talking about God and to end the day doing the same. It should begin to come naturally, rather than being perceived as a duty or task. And if we are not there yet, the first thing we need is to pray for and develop an intimate relationship with God for ourselves.

Needless to say, the more time we spend doing countless things from our to-do lists, the less time we are inclined to spend with God, hanging out with him, getting to know him and enjoying that intimacy. Therefore, as I indicated in the previous chapter, we must declutter our lives to have enough time to nurture relationship with God and enjoy His peace and rest. As mothers, we have plenty of work and energy-draining tasks to do, so it's essential that we enjoy the rest God gives us when we go to Him to recharge our batteries.

Some of the most energy-draining areas in my mom-life, are the areas of disciplining and correction of attitudes and behavior. Having to repeat the same correction or be consistent in giving consequences can drain my mental capacity. This does not really get any easier with each passing stage, as the life issues tend to become more complicated and the numbers and types of things that influence their minds increase and widen. In the following chapter, I will look at the biblical perspective on doing what is right in God's eyes. Children need to be taught God's Word. They also need to be guided into applying His Word into their lives. I will explore the topic of training kids in righteousness and disciplining them in the chapter below.

CHAPTER 3
TRAINING IN RIGHTEOUSNESS AND DISCIPLINE

All Scripture is God-breathed and is useful for
teaching, rebuking, correcting and training in
righteousness, so that the servant of God may be
thoroughly equipped for every good work.
— 2 Timothy 3:16-17

What comes to your mind when you hear the word "training"? To me, the first thought that pops up is something that takes a lot of time and hard work. Training our children in the path of righteousness so they learn to choose ways that please God is time consuming and involves hard work. Training our children in righteousness must be founded on using God's Word for teaching, correcting and rebuking (2 Timothy 3:16) so those precious little ones are guided to live their lives in a manner that pleases God. Training takes place when we put the Word into practice! Related to training is also the very popular topic (or unpopular, depending on how you see it) of disciplining children. I'll share what discipline means to me from my personal experience as a mother a little later.

First, we must begin by agreeing on this point: training in righteousness is not something magical that transforms our children in a few weeks' or even months' time. Rather, it is a time-consuming, energy-draining, and sometimes disheartening exercise that a mama (of little and teenage kids) needs to do pretty much every single day of her life. Sounds exhausting? Yes, it is. There's no beating around the bush here. Yet, the rewards are also great when we see our children making progress in an area where they have been struggling. Once again, I would like to emphasize the importance of investing time and just "being there" with, and for, our children, because that's the most natural way to give them the necessary training. We can't outsource this crucial parental responsibility to outsiders, like Sunday school teachers or other caregivers. Outside caregivers can be an important source of biblical truth and can enforce discipline, but they are not meant to provide the individualized attention and training that must be received from a mother, who is designed to know her child best.

What is righteousness? According to the Strong's Concordance, the original Greek word for righteousness is *dikaiosy'ne,* which refers to what is deemed right by the Lord (after His examination), i.e. what is approved in His eyes.[1] Our goal is to train our children to do what is right in God's eyes. Since God's Word reveals to us what is right or wrong, we train them according to the values laid out by God, in His Word. The state of righteousness (being righteous) does not occur because of what we do, but comes through faith in Jesus Christ (a study of the book of Romans would clarify this very important concept). So then, what is the purpose of this training, since we are made righteous only through faith anyway? Training in righteousness brings children to God's Word, which teaches them about God's ways. As they see them how different their actions are from God's perfect standard, they are shown that turning to Christ as the only way they can lead a righteous life (Romans 3:20). In other words, faith in Christ is what we need to teach them from the earliest age. We could easily give our children a set of rules by teaching Bible stories, highlighting truths, and telling them the way to live. But then...what happens? Unless we take the time to correct them and lead them to Christ every time, they will grow up knowing God's Word only as a list of requirements to follow. Living this way will create discouragement and frustration because they will be unable to "succeed" in this kind of faith.

Christian parents have a godly mandate: we are to train up our children in the Word of God (Proverbs 22:6). As Christian mothers, we've been given the Great Commission from Jesus, right in our own homes. We are to disciple our children and teach them to obey in everything (Matthew 28:20). We cannot know when a child receives Jesus and is assured of salvation. Only God knows what is in a person's heart (Acts 1:24; Romans 8:27). So, we are called to disciple—to show our children the way of Jesus, teach them about Him, walk with them humbly, and demonstrate the reality of an intimate fellowship with God. Our discipleship mandate requires that we train our children to know God and to live a life that pleases Him.

What does this training in righteousness look like, practically? Let's look at 2 Timothy 3:16 again. God's Word is used "to teach, rebuke, correct and train in righteousness." I use this verse practically. The three methods listed—teaching, rebuking, correcting—are, in fact, the very tools that mothers can use for training in righteousness. Our children need help in knowing what God's Word says about the things they encounter in their lives. They need us to hold their hands and guide them in the right course of action and behavior, rather than leaving them on their own to figure out those things. Training them requires perseverance because often we must repeat the same things again and again to remind them of the right course of action. Our prayer is that the repetition becomes less frequent as they grow older!

Spending quality time with our children is very important, but I think as far as training them up in the right ways of behavior is concerned, quantity of time spent is of paramount importance. Let me explain. The more time we spend with them, even we are just hanging out, the more readily we can observe their personalities, seeing all the good, bad, and ugly. With firsthand knowledge of them, we can tackle each difficulty as it arises. Individualized correction and personal teaching moments cannot really happen at a Sunday school or even in regular family devotional times.

Let's look at the principle of quantity time through the lens of a few examples. Keep in mind that if you are home with your two kids all day, you will likely experience an emotional roller coaster ride—from peace, joy, laughter, and excitement, to boredom, frustration, anger, lack of self control, and guilt then back to peace, joy, laughter—phew, what a day! Now in that whole time several things may have happened to cause those emotions. Here is a scenario: your five-year -old son is getting very bored and decides he needs to bring some excitement into his life. He sees his three-year-old sister, who is quietly playing with her toy teapot in the play kitchen. He eyes the teapot. He wants some tea too. He needs it now. He goes over to his sister and snatches the teapot from her hands.

I hardly need to write what happens next! Maybe you are getting the lunch ready in your own kitchen when suddenly you have to step into the mess that is happening in the play kitchen! The temptation is to yell to bring this situation "under control." You might think, "Oh no! Not again, it's always the same thing. Is there anything else in my life, besides managing these fighting kids?" But next time, pause for a moment. Think instead, "This very kitchen mess is the perfect training ground for raising responsible, considerate children! I've been placed here, in this very moment, with these children, to deal with this mess."

The less time we see our kids each day, the fewer opportunities we have for teaching, correcting, or rebuking as necessary. Except for homeschoolers, it's impossible for us to have our school-aged kids with us all the time. But homeschooled or not, it's healthy for kids to have other adult contacts besides mom and dad from time to time, such as grandparents, aunts, uncles or other trusted adults. However, as much as possible, especially when the kids are in their fundamental childhood development stages, it's good for mom to be with them to observe their little personalities developing and growing.

You may think training in righteousness, by being with your children, sounds nice and easy on paper, but when the reality of the day hits, it's a different story. Know this—I am writing from the battlefield. I know what a day with fussy kids looks like, because I live that every day! Correcting another bad attitude or refereeing one more fight is exhausting. And sometimes we don't even know what to do or how to correct a behavior or attitude. That's why we need to go back to the Word often. So, the next time Peter wants to have song number one from the CD playing in the car and Ruth wants nothing but song number six, you can pray and seek God's wisdom. And perhaps God will point you to a specific verse. He did that for me the other day. It was Philippians 2:4. "Each of you should look not only to your own interests, but also to the interests of others." You never know, one of them may finally turn it around due to hearing God's Word at the right moment. Pray that God would speak to their little hearts the next time, and every time, with verses they've heard already.

It's true: children are like sponges. They are fast learners when it comes to picking a language or learning to climb stairs. But when it comes to learning from mistakes concerning a sinful behavior, sometimes I wonder! I think they often do know what is right and wrong, but choosing to do right is another matter. Isn't it the same for you and me? We may know God's Word, but choosing to do it is another story. I know I fail...quite often! I thank my God that He is so patient with me, persevering and not giving up on me. In the same way, I am also called to persevere in teaching, correcting and rebuking my children for their own good. Therefore, *perseverance* is key to training them in the department of morally and socially responsible behavior, founded upon the values that are important to our family. Even if we have to correct and remind them of the right thing to do again and again, it is ultimately worth it.

Another key ingredient for training children is *patience*. Oh my, I've learned a thing or two about being patient since having children! Sometimes, I need to remind myself, daily, to be patient when my four-year-old asks me for the tenth time about taking his Legos to preschool. I have to tell myself, "This is a phase which is part of the growing process for three or four-year-olds—they just love to go on asking the same thing!" This phase, too, shall pass! I need to get through each stage with patience, and give my child grace. In a similar way, God is patient with me and gives me grace, even though I keep asking Him for the same thing over and over when He gives me, "No," for an answer. I'm thankful that that He doesn't just give up and go away, or get angry and yell at me. Rather, He is patient and perseveres with me, allowing me to mature at my own pace.

Correcting and rebuking our children using God's Word not only takes time, but also wisdom, prayer, and confrontation! We pray for wisdom to know how to correct our children when necessary. This wisdom can sometimes require us to confront bad behavior directly. We might often need to be the "bad guy" in the family. Confrontation is something many parents avoid because of the fear that their children may not like them.

However, there is no reason to be afraid. Our children will one day thank us for giving them boundaries to live by.

Children become more secure individuals when they know that their parents care enough to guide them in the right path, even if they may not always appreciate the correcting at the time. I am so thankful that my parents cared enough for me to correct me and were very strict when needed. Their intervention saved me from a lot of potentially heartbreaking and dangerous situations. As a parent myself now, I can see that my kids come to me as their safe haven and comfort, in spite of getting rebuked or disciplined for misbehaviors. God's Word says: "no discipline seems pleasant at the time, but painful. Later on, however, it produces a harvest of righteousness and peace for those who have been trained by it" (Hebrews 12:11). The harvest of righteousness comes when we patiently persevere in training and disciplining our children according to God's Word.

Disciplining

This is a topic that is very close to my heart as I am passionate about raising my children to be Christ followers. Discipline is a biblical concept and we see this talked about and applied throughout the Bible in various contexts such as parenting, church conduct, and God's way of dealing with the children of Israel (Proverbs 29:17; Ephesians 6:1-9; Deuteronomy 8:5; Proverbs 23:13; Hebrews 12:5-11; Revelation 3:19; Psalm 94:12-14; Joshua 7:10-26; Judges 21:5-12). There are several good Christian books on disciplining children, providing guidelines and practical application points (See Appendix 1). Therefore, it is not my intention to write another book on disciplining children. I am neither super qualified, other than being the mother of five kids, nor is it the focus of this book. However, I do feel strongly about this topic and want to share a few of the more important things I have personally learned about disciplining children.

Discipline is a hot topic and is understood in a variety of ways by different people. There may not be a right or wrong answer in your eyes, but after some research, it's quite clear to me that discipline does have to do with *training, instruction* and *punishment*. A topical study of discipline in the Bible reveals some distinct characteristics of "true discipline." Those are (a) the motivation for discipline must be love for the recipient (Proverbs 3:11,12; Hebrews 12: 7-10), and (b) the ultimate

45

purpose of discipline is restoration by God so the recipient might become who God has created him/her to be (Hebrews 12:11; 1 Peter 5:10).

One of the reasons why discipline is not considered a positive word in today's society is that many people understand it as primarily punishment. Many a consequence is handed out by parents, without the child ever getting a chance to understand why he was given a consequence in the first place. Or some parents loathe the word discipline (once again, associating it with punishment) and as a result go into lengthy discussions with their young children. Rather than giving age-appropriate consequences for bad behavior, some parents talk and talk, ultimately letting the child get away with the wrong action or behavior.

We, the mamas, as gatekeepers of our children's overall well-being, must keep in mind that discipline needs to be done because we love our little ones. Love is part of all good discipline. At all times, but especially after an appropriate consequence has been meted, we must reaffirm our love for our children. Ross Campbell, in his book *How to Really Love Your Child* states, "Love and discipline cannot be separated, and punishment is a very small part of discipline. Making a child feel loved is the first and most important part of good discipline."[2] I have strived to take this truth to heart. I always try to not scold my children in a way that will embarrass them in front of other people. The hurts that a child feels when publicly rebuked turn into very deep scars that journey well through adulthood. However, we also need to provide our children with boundaries within which they are taught to walk for their own good.

I've noticed that my children, even during the "wannabe independent troublesome threes" phase, have somehow always been able to sense that boundaries which are placed around them are meant to keep them out of danger, trouble, heartache and embarrassment. It's been as if God Himself has spoken to their souls, telling them that He loves them so much that He has put His helper, in the form of their mom, to guard them and protect them! I am not implying here that they never behave badly, because they do and sometimes it's more than my patience can handle, but they do know why rules and boundaries are in place. Christian educators and authors Nicky and Sila Lee observe that, "discipline involves teaching, guiding and training, as well as correcting – with unpleasant consequences, if necessary.

Putting appropriate boundaries around our child's behavior lays a good foundation on which character, self-discipline and maturity can be built."[3] So, yes, good discipline sometimes feels unpleasant, but we should always keep the end in mind, which is a harvest of righteousness and peace (Hebrews 12:11).

If disciplining kids is a biblical concept, and a practically important one, then why do so many parents shy away from doing it? I think a part of the reason could be that there is a general negative association with the word discipline in today's society. Many parents seem to worry that their kids won't like them or that they would not be "fun" parents if they discipline their kids too much. Many parents decide that disciplining is downright exhausting. Although I agree with that statement wholeheartedly, and admit that discipline, especially when there is more than one kid to train, is not a particularly fun thing to do, I must point out here that disciplining should not be attempted through our own strength. Our batteries will run low in the blink of an eye! We need wisdom from the Lord at every moment. From 1 Thessalonians 5:17, we see that "pray continually," may also be applied as a disciplining motto!

Lack of discipline in children can be observed very commonly today. So many kids lack manners and basic respect, have no established routines, and exhibit frequent crankiness. I have heard a few parents complaint that they are so overwhelmed by "difficult behavior" in their child that they give up on having more kids. Children, who are supposed to be regarded as a blessing, a reward from the Lord (Psalm 127:3), are gradually viewed as inconvenient and tiresome.

Though there are days when I'm exhausted and weary from doing the same chores, and correcting the same mistakes, I've found it's important to persevere in the discipline department. It is especially important to be consistent at the times when I have the least desire to do it. I'm not saying that I've got it all together—no way—but I have learned a few things that do seem to work with my young kids, those in the little years up through the end of elementary school age. Here are my key take-home discipline points:

- Establish boundaries: teach kids the clear no-go areas and to respect those boundaries. Teach them that, though you are always there for them, you need time for yourself, and with your husband, and they are to respect that.

- Give age-appropriate instructions: under one-year-olds should not experience any form of harsh disciplining because they can't learn anything that way, whereas stubborn five-year-olds are unlikely to respond to gentle requests. You'll need to tailor the consequences for disobedient and defiant acts according to age, maturity and personality. Once again, pray for wisdom. God, who disciplines His children for their own good, will not ignore your request.

- Follow through with consequences: There should be no empty threats. Kids are smart. They can be quite manipulative and are often trying to test the limits of your patience. So, if you cannot follow through with a consequence realistically, then do not mention it. For instance, saying the following is a bad idea because you are unlikely to abandon your child and it would be horrible if you did: "Stop crying or I will just leave you in this store."

- Be consistent: Ideally, others who are caring for your children, especially at home, should follow the same discipline approach, so as not to confuse them. Let me clarify, I don't mean this in terms of rebuking, because I believe any corporal form of punishment, such as spanking, should be carried out only by the father or mother. What I say here is in reference to eating and sleeping habits. If the rule established by parents allows a child to have dessert only after finishing her dinner, then caregivers should enforce this rule too, when the parents are not there.

• Persevere: Don't give up on the rules that you have started establishing. Keep holding children to the same standards, with the same consequences as long as the rules bear fruit and make logical sense. It will be so worth it when you experience the fruit of peace that comes along with it.

In the process of disciplining, we should not nag and exasperate our children (Colossians 3:21). I am reminding myself of this as much I am telling you. Pick your battles, because not every argument needs to be had. For example, if your little three-year-old wants to wear the same polka dot dress, three days in a row, then let her do it! This disciplining business is no doubt a tiring business, but there is no real formula to produce disciplined kids other than to spend time with them, get to know them and their personalities, and persevere in guiding them on the right path. There will be lots of trials and errors here, as well as heartaches and little breakthroughs. Just don't give up. Go to God for whatever you need.

Husband and Wife - United in Purpose

I cannot leave this chapter without bringing attention to one very important thing. Before we can invest in our kids spiritually, we need to evaluate how we are doing on the marital unity front. You might be wondering how much being united with your husband has to do with spiritual investment in your *children.* The answer is quite a bit. It is, in fact, the very basis of raising children. Through the prophet Malachi, God said that He made a husband and wife one, in flesh and in spirit, because He was seeking godly offspring (Malachi 2:15). Marriage is created by God Himself so that a man and a woman can come together and become one spiritually and physically (Genesis 2:24, Malachi 2:15). This means that a husband and wife should not only come together in sexual union to produce a child, but they must also be united spiritually, following God and His ways concerning different aspects of their lives, particularly in the area of raising their kids together. Why? God engineered this as the best way for His people to fulfill their purpose of raising godly children for Him.

The basis for raising godly children, as we saw in Malachi 2:15, is being "one" as parents. Being united in purpose is of utmost important if we want to raise children that follow and obey God. Being united does not mean that we have to agree with our husbands on every single point. Rather, unity comes through (1) the wife's attitude of submission to the husband's authority, as the head of the family, and (2) the willingness of both parties to establish rules and routines together, for the benefit of everyone. I know there are many husbands who have failed in this area, by not following through with their responsibilities at home, but I cannot speak to them. I can only encourage you, if your husband is one of them, to pray every day that God works in his heart and gives you the right attitude toward him and that He provides wisdom for you to know how to deal with differences respectfully.

It is God's grace alone that will lead our children to know Christ, and He can bring them to Himself in spite of our shortcomings. However, all children should see the love of Christ being modeled by their parents. When there is lack of unity between parents in raising them, children do not respond as well to discipline and training in righteousness. If there are disagreements between mom and dad, kids need to see their parents praying and asking for forgiveness, from the Lord and from each other. Children learn about the fruits of the Holy Spirit of God—"love, joy, peace, patience, kindness, goodness, gentleness, faithfulness and self-control"—from their parent's attitude and behavior towards one another (Galatians 5:22-23, NLT).

I know my sons and daughters are watching the way I act towards my husband, especially when he says something I do not agree with. Yet, God can help me to use even my disagreement as a training ground for my children. Let's imagine a scenario: one of the kids wants to go and get himself a drink while my husband is reading a Bible story, but the rule is that he must sit quietly and listen during Bible reading. The rest of the family is paying good attention to the reading and sitting quietly. The child says he is thirsty and looks rather desperate, at least to me. The softie that I am towards the kids, I think it should be okay for him to quickly go and get a drink, provided he doesn't cause any distractions. But my husband tells him not to do so until the reading time is over, say in about seven minutes. I have a choice. I may stand by my husband's decision or argue with him and let the child get his way. I do have my own opinion, but in order to respect the authority of my husband as the leader of the family, I set aside my point of view. This may sound like a trivial example, but disunity in small matters often leads to disunity in bigger matters and more importantly, standing against him would demonstrate lack of respect towards the leader of our family.

If the husband and wife are united in the discipline department, the kids get a consistent message on how to behave which helps them understand big, difficult concepts such as submission and authority. On the other hand, if the husband and wife are not united in disciplining methods, kids will easily see the division and are encouraged try to find loopholes to rebel against authority. Sounds manipulative, but if you have kids you will know that your cute little offspring are indeed capable of disobedience, rebellion, and deception.

Let's look at another example where unity between parents may be a challenge: a father says his daughter, Amy, must come down for breakfast by 7am to eat or, if she does not, she gets no food before the school bus comes. Seeing poor Amy's sad face, Mother goes soft on her little dear, getting breakfast for her no matter what time she comes down. What sort of message is young Amy getting here? She knows Mommy is there to get her breakfast either way, so what is the point of stressing over Daddy's rules? She and her mother are both happy as she dashes off to the bus. The problem is that Mommy's behavior undermines the authority of Daddy. This seemingly small occurrence demonstrates inconsistency to children and gives them mixed messages about living under authority and taking responsibility.

When the husband and wife are on the same page "doctrinally", it means that they agree on their beliefs and interpretations concerning the God and the Bible. If this is the case, then they will give consistent teaching to their children, even if schedules prevent them from studying the

Bible together. On the other hand, if a husband and wife do not see eye-to-eye on specific topics, it is wise to pray about those issues together and study the Scriptures and come to agreement, rather than teaching different interpretations to kids. However, there will be many gray areas where the Bible does not give clear answers and parents may have different viewpoints about them. In such instances, the way parents respond to each other concerning those differences is vital. Do wife and husband "lovingly" and "respectfully" disagree, or are loud fights and flying objects more the norm? Kids see everything and they need to learn it's very healthy to ask questions and it's all right to have different opinions. The manner in which debate is conducted is very important. I don't mean to be preachy about this, but I speak from my experience that kids observe everything. I have been rude, and not at all gentle, with my husband on more than one occasion and, to my utter shame, found the kids watching me! How disappointing. Thankfully, I know there is a way out of this shame and disappointed feeling—going as quickly as possible to the Lord to repent! Likewise, I can repent and be united with my husband again.

It is beyond the scope of this book to talk about fostering marital unity in detail. However, I would really encourage you to study the Bible on the topic of marriage and husband-wife relationships. There are plenty of passages in the Bible about this issue. You might select this subject for the next topic of your quiet time? You may also choose to read biblically-based Christian books on marriage. There so many good reads available, it may seem that there are too many to choose just one! For your convenience, I've listed a few books I can recommend in Appendix 2. Investing in your marriage is important. We start with relationship with God first, and other relationships like marriage and children must be nurtured as well.

CHAPTER 4
INVESTING IN THEIR
EMOTIONAL SECURITY

We were gentle among you, like a mother
caring for her little children.
— 1 Thessalonians 2:7

A mother's work is never finished. How true this is, on so many different levels. A mother who seeks the best for her child's all-around development is always at work, making sure her child feels safe, secure, loved and that he or she meets their creative, intellectual, physical and social potential. However, with limited time, mental energy, and physical capabilities, mothers often feel overwhelmed trying to do it all, having to wear different hats. Thankfully, a mother's work does not have to be overwhelming, in order for her children to be healthy and happy. The abundant life found by faith in Jesus Christ gives peace, rest and hope in every circumstance. The Lord Jesus' sacrifice on the cross is a finished work and His resurrection provides security in every situation.

Mothers of little ones have the assurance that Jesus is able to carry all of their burdens and that His love is enough to fill the emotional tank of their children (Matthew 11:28; 1 Peter 5:7). This same Lord also shows us how we can best support our children in their physical development, because He has created them, and He knows them best. If I believe that He died so that I can live, then I ought to really live, fully secure in His love for me and for my children. This knowledge should free me from the busyness we see among mothers who want their kids do every possible activity in order to develop. If I love my children with God's love, not coming from my flesh, but from His Spirit, I can support them in their all-around development without pressuring them or comparing them to other kids. My primary purpose is to lead my kids to Christ so they can know His love and seek His will for their lives. Therefore, knowing Christ and depending on Him is the foundation of both (a) our ability to invest in the emotional and physical development of our kids and (b) the result of that investment, as seen in our kids.

Here at the outset of this chapter, I have a task for you. I would like you to read the verse in Romans 12:1-2.

"Therefore, I urge you, brothers and sisters, in view of God's mercy, to offer your bodies as a living sacrifice, holy and pleasing to God—this is your true and proper worship. Do not conform to the pattern of this world, but be transformed by the renewing of your mind. Then you will be able to test and approve what God's will is—his good, pleasing and perfect will."

This, I believe, is a crucial verse in our lives as mamas, if we are to live out the mandate of raising children God's way. There is no way we can do this task if we are still doing things that seem right because everyone else around is doing so. We cannot expect to know what God's will is for our children if we are always trying to do what the other moms at school are doing for their children, like enrolling a daughter in ballet class because Lisa's mom did so last week. Dear friends, we must stay out of the pattern of doing things because the world does them. The command in Romans 12:2 pertains to all aspects of our lives as women in marriage, work, parenting, fashion, and homemaking. The list could go on and on. We should work, or not work, as we follow God's will for our lives. We can enroll our child in a violin class because it meets her heart's desire, instead of doing it to keep up socially or intellectually with other kids.

We can live free, because Christ's rule sets us free from the rule of this world. Walking to the beat of a different drummer instead of copying the world gives glory to God. Being set apart also arouses curiosity in a few people along the way as to why and how we are different from the rest. We can and should live differently as Christians. Instead of chasing all that the world is offering, we can draw wisdom from just one source, God Himself, which allows us to invest the very best in our children. Drawing from the Lord, Who is an infinite source, provides us with the ability to *build emotional security* into our children without getting overwhelmed, frazzled and discouraged.

At the start of this chapter, I pointed out a verse from 1 Thessalonians where Paul describes a mother as gentle and caring. These traits are gifts of God, sort of like mommy genes. Even on days when I do not feel gentle or when I am wearied by my children, God has hard-wired these characteristics into my deepest being so that my children are able to see and feel them, in spite of my attitude! This is a very special bond that has been created by God, which is why children are most responsive to a mother's touch and care right from the very beginning of life.

That very special bond forms the basis of strong emotional security in a child that allows them to weather difficult seasons of life, whether we realize it or not. However, this God-given bond, if not nurtured, can also bring despair in a child's, and eventually an adult's, soul.

Psychological Research

Psychological researchers have noted a relationship between emotional security and child behavior. Emotional security is what we might think of as peace or confidence; it's having the inner resources to confront new and threatening situations. Psychologist Abraham Maslow proposed that understanding of emotional security is gained by studying its opposite: insecurity. He described an insecure person as someone that "perceives the world as a threatening jungle and most human beings as dangerous and selfish; feels rejected and isolated, anxious and hostile; is generally pessimistic and unhappy; shows signs of tension and conflict; tends to turn inward; is troubled by guilt-feelings; has one or another disturbance of self-esteem; tends to be neurotic; and is generally egocentric and selfish."[4] An emotionally secure person would not be defined by the same characteristics or would exhibit them to a lesser degree. Maslow viewed in every insecure person the continual, never-dying longing for security. Security, coming from a sense of belonging and acceptance, is an innate desire in each one of us. No doubt this desire begins very early on in life.

Secular academic research and the Bible agree on this point: mothers, like you and me, play an important role in giving children the security they need in order to become emotionally healthy and secure adults one day. After all, none of us would really want our children to look like the insecure person described by Dr. Maslow! Psychological research has shown that some of the most intense emotions children will experience arise during the formation, the maintenance, the disruption, and the renewal of attachment relationships.[5] That is why it's only natural for children to feel secure when their moms are around and are "there for them".

A mother's presence might however, take different forms in different ages in a child's life. A younger child may need his mother to be around in a different way as compared to an older child. However, emotional security is built and maintained by the presence of the mother, or father, or main attachment person, whenever there is a need.[6],[7] Younger, securely-attached children derive their security from the conviction that the mother, or attachment figure, is in relative *physical* proximity, and is available when needed. Older children derive their feeling of security from the idea that, even if not available at the moment, they can count on their mothers when needed. Researchers say that a securely attached child is a child that feels emotionally secure because of a good attachment with the mother.[8]

Note here that, although attachment comes from the existence of a strong bond between the mother and the child, a distinction needs to be made between clinginess and attachment. When a child is clingy to his mama to the point that the mama is hardly able to finish a sentence, it is not necessarily a case of a strong attachment between the mother and child. Good attachment arising out of the bond between a mother and child is able to create emotionally secure children and clinginess in a child could actually indicate something different. A child that is not secure in the quality and quantity of his mother's presence may tend to get very clingy whenever he gets a moment with the mother. Have you wondered why an older child gets quite clingy, and might even behave badly, when there's a new baby in the home? Or why a whiny three-year-old will just not leave mother's side when she's trying to have a coffee and chat with a friend? Although these are not instances of bad behavior or signs of an emotional insecurity per se, they do help in understanding how a child responds to any change, real or felt, in his life. These behaviors maybe glimpses of your child's heart's cry for your attention and for his need to feel you're "present" in his life. These sorts of instances are likely to be magnified the more time you spend away from your children, especially if they are young. In this context, each of us can examine the busyness our lives and work that takes us away from home, especially if we notice a rather long phase of clinginess. We might just uncover surprising truths indicating that our absence, physical or emotional, is functioning as a hindrance to our children, preventing them from enjoying a good and healthy emotional security.

However, I would like to also note that the type of clinginess mentioned above should not be confused with the phase of "separation anxiety" that a child/baby goes through, which is a normal part of the growing up process. According to *Psychology Today* magazine[9], separation anxiety usually occurs when babies are between eight and fourteen months old. The first six months or so, a baby does not have a sense of danger in his normal environment. However, as he starts to develop, he may become more aware of the changes in his environment and begin to fear whenever something is unusual. Parents are usually the source of safety for the child. So, every time the parent leaves the baby, who does not have a sense of time or understand that parents will return, he feels threatened and frightened. This is particularly true when he's away from the familiar home setting. If you are a new mother, and experience your baby crying hysterically even if you go to the bathroom for a few minutes, don't be too alarmed! The world is still okay and you are not a miserable, failure of a parent!! Your child is just showing you that he "misses" you because he has a special bond with you. Two out of my five children have had quite a strong separation anxiety phase, which lasted a good year, if not more. The other three had lesser ones, as thankfully they had more siblings around! I used to cry out in desperation, wondering if the phase would ever end. It did. Afterward, the kids became quite secure and independent. Today, they are very happy to be around different people or be with any trusted person—friends, neighbors, family—without my husband and me because they know they will eventually be reunited with their parents.

Clinginess shown by an older child, past the usual separation anxiety phase, can be disturbing, annoying, and make a mother want to join in the crying! Sometimes the clinginess indicates insecurity or an unmet emotional need that can be addressed when detected. For whatever reason, when expressions of emotional insecurity creep up in a child, it can effect the child's ability to tolerate frustration.[10] When young children feel insecure in their most basic attachment relationships, like with their parents, they tend to express it by acting out in their preschool or school. A preschool child who *feels* a lack of love, attention, and care from his parents will tend to get more easily frustrated in group activities and may be more likely to hit or punch other kids. A school-aged child may start bullying other kids, letting out frustration he feels from a real or perceived lack of love, attention, and respect at home.

Parents often believe that they give a lot of love, attention, care and respect to their kids, which may be completely true. However, it's important to find out why children are begging for attention and whether any basic emotional need is unmet. In order to determine this, we need to go back to the basic theme of this book once again—the investment of our time in our children's lives. Spending time with them to find out who they are and what they need.

Biblical Perspective

According to the Word of God, we see that emotional security comes, not because of who we are and what we can do for ourselves, but rather because of *Who God is*. Thankfully, with the help of the Holy Spirit, we can emulate some of God's wonderful character traits and build emotional security in our own children. Let's look at some of the characteristics of God that make us secure individuals who can live without fear of other people, their opinions, or outside circumstances.

God is Love (1 John 4:16)

"Perfect love drives out fear" (1 John 4:18). I can have confidence to parent with absolute security, knowing God loves my children and me and that He will protect us. God supplies me with the love I need so I can love my children even when I feel angry and upset. He teaches me to live fearlessly, becoming the defender of my children and learning to love them His way, rather than how others expect me to love them. For example, I grew up in the Indian culture where it is almost unthinkable that a little child will sleep in her own cot and not share a bed with her parents. Becoming a parent myself, and having lived away from my cultural origins for many years, I see things differently. Now it's my husband's and my choice, together, that we don't share a bed with our kids. I have had one or two eyebrows being raised concerning this matter, with some openly doubting how a loving mother can leave her child to sleep in another room. My answer is simply this: I leave my children in God's hands and therefore do not need to raise my children dictated by cultural norms. God's love also directs the choices I make for my kids with respect to school, activities, nutrition, clothing, sleep training, room decoration etc. that are not be driven by fear of what others will think or say!

God is Faithful (1 Thessalonians 5:24)

Throughout the Bible, we read about God's faithfulness. A mother by nature is, I suppose, faithful to her children. The attachment to her children leads a mother to feel a deep sense of faithfulness toward them. What are some of the ways of being faithful, in a practical sense? Mothers can be faithful by praying every day for her children—for their salvation and obedience to the Lord, for the different situations they face in life, and for their health. Part of showing faithfulness to children is keeping promises to them. For example, if a mother promises to spend an afternoon doing crafts with her kids, it is important to do it. Faithfulness is expressed by standing with them when they face tough situations in preschool or school, or at the park. Mothers need a lot of help from the Lord to follow through on faithfulness. It's true that fidelity is an innate characteristic in a mother, but true faithfulness must be cultivated by making consistent choices to *be* faithful.

God is Trustworthy (1 Chronicles 5:20, Psalm 112:7,8)

We read in many wonderful stories from the Old Testament about how God helped His people and answered their prayers whenever they put their trust in him. Psalm 112:7,8 also says that we can be secure and not fear any bad news when we trust in God. Trusting is something we do, but what does it say about God? It reveals a very important truth about the character of God, that He is *trustworthy.* We trust in him because He is worthy of our trust. We can absolutely rely on Him to come through, to keep His promises, to rescue us, to be there for us. What about me? Am I trustworthy? Can my children always rely on me to protect them, to keep my promises, to provide meals for them, to be there for them when they need me?

God is Ever-Present (Psalm 46:1)

God is always present. Okay, He is God. True. So, He can be everywhere to look upon us, to help us, to rescue us. We are limited to some degree here by our humanness. I cannot be there for each of my children or witness each and every thing that happens to them. However, the question I need to ask myself is: how much am I present in their lives? A younger child will no doubt have a different need for a mama as compared to an older child. The baby needs his mother. He needs the physical touch, soft caresses, cuddles, and milk from his mama. Call me old-fashioned, but I do believe this to be true. If the mother must work outside the home because there is no other way of providing for the family, then it's understandable that the baby must be left with another caregiver. However, it's God's design for mother and baby to be together, at least in the beginning

stages of the little one's life (1 Thessalonians 2:7; Isaiah 49:15).

As a child grows, she needs to know that her mother is there for

her, to provide healthy meals, to be there when she comes home

from school, to support her development in all ways, to show an

active interest in her schoolwork and friends, and more.

Family builds the Foundation of Emotional Security

The foundation of emotional security is built even as

a baby cries in hunger and the mother is there to nurse her

or give her the bottle, together with soothing cuddles. Of

course, there are times, as a mother, when you need a break

and you are not jeopardizing the emotional heath of your child

if you are unable to give her each and every feeding. Later,

the secure foundation is maintained and nurtured when the

mother is there to nourish her preschooler or school-aged

children with healthy snacks and a restful downtime when

they come back home. Never underestimate the power of

those routines, the importance of the little things you do for

your own children; they work to build and maintain a strong

foundation of emotional security.

A mother's relationship with her child is key to establishing healthy emotional security in the youngster. In addition, some other factors are important to children: a well-functioning family and quality time with dad, made possible by encouraged, built-up husbands.

A Well-Functioning Family

We hear of TV shows called *Modern Family*, we know countless families that are "blended" having been brought together after divorce, and there are increasing numbers of families started by homosexual couples. The Bible, on the other hand, gives very specific explanations of God's plans for a well-functioning family. God is the creator of family, ancient or modern. In Genesis 1:27-28, we see the first family being formed, and also given a purpose: "So God created man in his own image, in the image of God he created him; male and female he created them. God blessed them and said to them, 'Be fruitful and increase in number; fill the earth and subdue it.'" The prophet Malachi also spoke the words of the Lord, "Didn't the Lord make you one with your wife? In body and spirit you are his. And what does he want? Godly children from your union. So guard your heart; remain loyal to the wife of your youth. 'For I hate divorce!' says the Lord, the God of Israel" (Malachi 2:15-16, NLT). From the above two passages, we can see the meaning and purpose woven by God for a family:

* The family is not just a creation, but also a reflection of who God is. Each individual—father, mother, daughter, and son—is made to reflect God's image. By seeing each of us, one can see a glimpse of God! Wow, isn't that huge! How often do I tell my children that truth? Not often enough. We're not all bad, you know. Before sin entered the world, we were actually perfect! Thankfully, God sent His Son to the broken, sinful world years after the entrance of sin into the world in order to change us and gradually conform us to His original creation. Little by little, He is polishing us, cleaning us of all the dirt and grime stuck to us, and wiping us clean to reveal Himself. Yes, it is taking some time because the dirt and grime seem to be quite stubborn, but it will happen eventually. We can encourage each of our family members by reminding ourselves of this very basic truth: we are made in God's

image, and we are all getting there eventually, after a detour of sin in life.

- Family starts with the union between a man and woman, in the form of marriage. And in this marriage, total loyalty is required. A husband and wife, faithful in thought and action towards one another is the basis of a healthy family.

- God's intent of this man-woman union is to produce children so as to carry on *His* name. We may call ourselves "Family Brown" or "Family Mueller" or "Family A, B, or C," but a Christian family ultimately bears the name of God. Our purpose in marriage is to bring forth offspring that will carry on the name and work of God.

A well-functional family (even with all its imperfections) is therefore paramount to raising kids that are emotionally secure in who they are, having received their identity from a father and mother who are united. I am in no way suggesting that emotionally secure kids come from a marriage where the mom and dad have never fought or argued. Far from it! After all, marriage, Christian or not, is comprised of two sinful people. Couples, even the most "united" ones, argue because each person wants to do things his or her way. Our kids need transparency in their family life. They will see parents arguing, but should also see them making up, asking for forgiveness, and forgiving. Marriage is a place where kids can see Christ's love in action, where daddy helps mommy by coming home early from work to take them out for an ice cream, so mommy can have some downtime after a long, busy week. Kids need to see that though mommy and daddy had a fight, they come together to pray and ask God to forgive them and help them to talk properly again.

One verse that has always stayed with me, helping in any conflict situation is this: "In your anger do not sin: do not let the sun go down while you are still angry, and do not give the devil a foothold" (Ephesians 4:26-27). For me, this means I should try to reconcile with my husband before I go to sleep. I don't want any bitterness creeping in and taking root in my heart even as I sleep. An angry heart is a fertile soil for the devil's work. Before I know it, I'm so angry that I start making up all possible negative scenarios in my mind, and I'm bitter and angry towards, not only my husband, but also the children, the dog, the babysitter, my neighbor, the next driver on the street…basically anyone that comes my way. That's why I need to make an effort to talk about the disagreements and settle them without delay, through humility, prayer and God's wisdom, so that a harmless quarrel or argument does not turn into a harmful, damaging, long-standing disagreement. My husband needs to do this too, but that is not in my hands. I am responsible for my part, and he is responsible for his.

Many children see their parents always fighting as "normal". The sad reality is that constant disharmony is crushing to a child's emotional well-being and usually results in some kind of spill-over into other areas of life in their teenage and adult years. Unresolved marital conflict that goes on and on can make children think that their security is threatened, and consequently they can experience feelings of insecurity. Psychologists Davies and Cummins explain that when exposed to marital conflict, children feel insecure and develop emotional and behavioral strategies to rapidly recover their sense of security.[11] This helps explain what we discussed earlier—how insecure children can become extremely whiny and clingy in preschool age, bully classmates in elementary school, and might take more drastic actions in their teenage years. Everyone develops coping mechanisms in response to daily conflict. If we don't invest the time in creating marital unity, it's our children who might suffer most as a result.

The overall home environment where the family lives also plays a role in fostering security in a child. One of the things I really appreciated in my childhood, and even teenage years, is that my mother was home when I came back from school, although I must confess my appreciation came much later in life. In childhood years, I took these things for granted. She was there waiting with nutritious and tasty snacks and was always the person to whom I could unburden myself. I realize now, as I endeavor to be home when my young ones come back from school and preschool, I am the one providing the atmosphere of security, a safe haven built up for the kids. Yes, there is often cranky behavior. Yes, there is some amount of grumpiness from one child or another. Yet as we continue this routine, I've learned to see the crankiness and grumpiness as ways the kids unburden themselves because they feel they have the freedom and security to "let it out". There's no doubt that it's hard work to manage the emotional drama of these little people and not let it get out of control.

Every family may have a different way of allowing its members unwind and feel relaxed. I know a very wise mom who somehow manages to create an amazingly peaceful atmosphere in her home, even with little children around. She uses candles, soft music, gentle words and lots of meaningful cuddles. I am sure this family has its fair share of conflicts, but the children are friendly, conversational and respectful, exuding a heart-warming sense of confidence, which is really a delight to experience. There is another friend who lets her kids unwind afterschool by playing with their favorite Lego creations or fire trucks. If the siblings' spats tend to get louder and louder, my friend often sends them to listen to an audiobook or to practice their musical instruments. I have never seen her shun any of her kids, rather she shows them that their disruptive behavior has consequences and it's in their best interest to change their activities. Because this is their routine, the kids often follow her instructions without even getting into an argument.

A peaceful environment at home gives children a desire to be home and consider it the place they want to run to for shelter. This is especially important in teenage years, when children do not necessarily consider their parents the coolest people around. In her book, *What is a Family?*, Edith Schaeffer writes about family being the shelter in a storm[12]. How important this message is! We would be wise to remember this daily and pray that God helps each of us to create a shelter, especially the mom and dad of the family.

A conscious effort on my part to maintain a peaceful atmosphere when my husband returns home from work goes a long way in strengthening the family bond, thus fostering emotional security in my children. How so? Very simple. When my husband comes home, it is to a peaceful environment where I don't immediately jump on him to take care of the screaming and fighting kids or to complain about how hard my day was. Rather, he gets to unwind properly. He is then able to give us all his full attention after he is recharged. He is able to read to the kids, we are all able to pray and read God's Word in peace and laugh and share things on our hearts together. All these things go a long way in creating strong bonds in a family where children are able to fully express themselves, without fear.

I understand making home feel like a safe haven might sound very theoretical and idealistic, whereas in reality every normal family does disagree, argue, and yell. I'm not condoning conflict in the home, but simply acknowledging this as a reality. Yet, with the help of our great God, family life does not always have to be like that. He can, and does, change our families, and us if only we ask him! If we don't aim for a peaceful environment, remembering to pray and make a conscious effort to create a peaceful family life, the chances are that we will not be able to experience it either.

In addition, striving to maintain an atmosphere of encouragement at home blesses everyone in the family. Unfortunately, I have witnessed families where everyone crushes one another's spirit. There is hardly a word of encouragement in a home like this because everyone wants to be right. I am sure many such families do not consciously try to tear each other down. However, a lot of unchecked and thoughtless words coming out do not help build up self-esteem in the other family members. In contrast, I have seen families where mom and dad offer words of encouragement and hope to their children and, having this model, the children also encourage their parents and siblings when they feel down. To me, this is God's love in action within a family. Our words have the power to build up or tear down. Being mindful of this power, we must teach our children to use words that are pleasant, positive, and motivating. Our words should focus on what is good and be delivered in a gentle way. Children need to be corrected every time a not-so-nice/hurtful word comes out of their mouths towards their siblings, parents, friends or anyone. In this way, children are trained to become mature and secure individuals who do not need to build their self-esteem by putting other people down.

As I have mentioned, my husband usually prays, reads the Bible, and puts the kids to bed, though maybe not every single day. Even though I am writing this book for moms, I need to highlight the importance of the role of dads in our kids' lives too. There is a connection between us mamas investing our lives in our children and the role that the dad plays in those kids' lives. How?

Firstly, we must *let* our husbands be the head of the family so that they can lead spiritually. Although many of us know that the husband as head is a biblical principle, often it is hard to practice it in everyday life. I have seen many a Christian wife completely take over the spiritual and physical raising of children, not even allowing her husband to lead. As we become spiritually mature, reading our Bibles every day, we can become a bit complacent. We may think we know things better than our husbands, and certainly when it comes to raising our children! After all, many of us left our jobs to stay at home and look after our precious flesh and blood. Our husbands may see the great jobs we do and take less hands-on responsibility with the kids. Though he is not as familiar with some of our methods, he certainly won't enjoy our criticisms, saying that he's not doing the job properly. We must remember that investing in our kids' lives does not mean that we are meant to be the ultimate authority. When a husband gives direction for the family, with his wife supporting him in this role, kids are given more security.

Secondly, we should actively encourage the relationship between our husbands and our kids. When we understand that we do not need to do everything ourselves, we can be free to let our husbands have bonding time with the kids. So, how about instead of doing the grocery shopping next time, send your husband and daughter to do the same. Even if he does not sound thrilled at the idea of picking up bananas, chicken, and paper towels, he might be more motivated at the idea of having some alone-time with his little girl. But please do weigh the moments. It's probably better not to ask a tired and weary husband to go do some shopping when all he wants to do is lay on the couch and watch football. You could ask him to do the shopping, and it would be an incentive if you ask him politely, with the added motivation of spending time with his child. Or you could encourage your husband to go out and have some fun—hiking, camping, face-painting, going to a movie, or eating out, one-on-one with one child to have some quality bonding time.

Thirdly, we must encourage our husbands and build them up. More often than not, a father-child relationship depends on the overall marriage relationship. Encouraging words from dads are life-changing. Kids thrive on that. A dad should be built up by words from the woman closest to him, the wife who will really encourage him, not just use empty words to boost his ego. A dad who is encouraged like this will share that encouragement with his children. Kindness from her father builds up the self-image of your little girl. A girl with a nurtured heart is more likely to stand up to peer pressure in teenage years. Affirmation from our closest relationships carry more weight than any motivational talk or feminist magazine can. A dad's encouraging pat and hopeful words will stay with a young boy. As he becomes an adult, the son will feel less of a need to prove his worth by working long hours, at the expense of having a normal family life.

A good friend's eight-year-old daughter was feeling rather low the other day because she felt the kids at school didn't want to play with her because of her skin color. No matter how much my friend tried telling her she was beautiful, the eight-year-old was not convinced. When her daddy came home from work, he sat his little girl on his knee and whispered, "You are my girl and I love you. God has made you so beautiful. You are Daddy's treasure." Tears rolled down her cheeks and she gave a big hug to her daddy and mommy. This wonderful and godly father, my friend's husband, invested his time in building his daughter up. I know his wife prays for him and tries to build him up with her words and deeds every single day.

Unconditional Love and Boundaries

The evening had ended badly. I had put the kids to bed not feeling happy. I did not even want to see one of them in particular. I had sent this child to bed without a good night kiss. All the whining and complaining had been too much for me to bear. I sat down to eat dinner on my own, put up my feet, and switched on the latest episode of *Downton Abbey*. My husband was out of town and I was feeling tired and angry at being left on my own to deal with grumpy, whiny kids. The television drama featuring the British aristocrats had barely started when I felt an inward nudge and heaviness in my heart. I knew I had to go to my sweet girl and settle our "issues" from the day. As I entered the room, she was still awake and unable to fall asleep. Apparently, she was feeling pretty much the same way I was, restless and sad. I sat by her bed and wanted to pray with her. My girl asked me whether I still loved her because I had looked so angry! I explained to her that my love for her would not increase or decrease because of her behavior. However, different behaviors would draw different responses and, because mommy was human, she also could get more angry than is good for anyone.

From my daughter's end, there had been instances of outright disobedience as well as some not so nice words. Thankfully, God forgives us when we go to him and say sorry and really want to change our behavior. I prayed then and there and asked God to forgive me for my anger. And soon after, my daughter prayed that God would forgive her for not listening to mommy and being a naughty girl. We hugged each other and felt a heavenly hug from our Father too.

The lesson I've learned is that, even though I love my children, I cannot overlook their sin as if nothing happened. If I did, I would not be submitting to God's design for me as a mother, which is to supervise the overall growth of my children. In the exercise of my authority as a parent, I must treat sin as sin. And sinning requires repentance. God's Word explicitly states that children must honor and obey their parents (Exodus 20:12; Colossians 3:20). Furthermore, just as the Lord disciplines the ones He loves (Proverbs 3:11-12), I must discipline my children because I love them. So many parents today seem afraid to discipline their children. I wonder why. Is it because they fear their kids won't love them if they punish them? Or is it because parents feel they cannot punish the very child they brought to this world in love? Or is it an underlying fear that their children will rebel at some point if they are told what to do?

It may seem to be a kind of a paradox, almost an oxymoron, to have the words "unconditional love" and "boundaries" linked together. You may think the two concepts don't really go together. On one hand, there is love with no conditions and on the other, the importance of boundaries to show mutual respect and have good behavior. The common understanding of unconditional love, even biblically, seems to be accepting someone completely—strengths, weaknesses, good behavior, bad behavior, all alike. I think this way of understanding the concept of unconditional love is only partially correct. God does love us unconditionally in that He has chosen us because of nothing that we have done. We have been saved by grace alone, even though we were yet sinners (Ephesians 2:8; Romans 5:8). This shows that God's saving of us is entirely an act of love, independent of how good or bad we have been. Think of the prodigal son and his father's heart. The father did not stipulate any condition for the son to come back to him. He could return to his father's house, and heart, falling into his outstretched arms.

In the same way, our Father in Heaven, who is our loving Father, loves us with an everlasting love (Jeremiah 31:3). When we fall, His kindness remains. In fact, He is there to pick us up. Because He loves us, He sent His Son to show us how to live and also to die for our sin. There is really no greater love than this (John 15:13). And it gets even better. Christ rose from the dead in order that those who believe in Him could live a new life by following and obeying Him, precisely because God loves us too much to leave us in the evil grips of sin.

There is no doubt that God loves us and that our forgiveness is assured when we turn to him (1 John 1:9). Yet His love for His people is not entirely without conditions, when we really dig into the Word. God does command us to obey him if we say we love him (John 15:9-10). Faith is also a condition for belonging to God, even if it is a gift given by Him. We need to still display and demonstrate faith.

God is perfectly holy and thus in absolute fairness, He cannot allow us to enter His presence with blemish and uncleanness. However, because of His great love for us He has given us boundaries within which we are to walk if we are to enjoy His presence one day. In this life, of course we will have good days and bad ones. We will soar. We will fly low. The important thing is to remain within the boundaries God has given us and heed His correction, every time He corrects us. How does he correct us? God works in us through His Holy Spirit, which can take the form of conviction directly through Scripture reading or through the words of a godly brother or sister.

In the light of how God "parents" His children, what does it mean to love our kids unconditionally, within the boundaries given, so they grow up being secure? Sally Clarkson, whose books have always brought a fresh air to my mothering, pointed out in her book *The Mission of Motherhood*, "a child who can go to her mother or father and reveal her inner heart and still feel accepted will feel secure enough to take risks and grow." [13]Our children must be allowed to express themselves. Self-expression starts young, and sometimes it is hard to appreciate the tantrums of a two-year-old. Emotional outbursts, handled well by the parent, allow the child his moment of "self expression," yet imparts the knowledge that there is someone to guide him when he is "being himself." Leniency with this kind of self-expression needs to be adjusted according to age. At every stage, the child must know who is in authority. I am not condoning the expression of parental authority by coercion, threats, yelling, or force in any way, but a child must know that the mom and dad are in control and responsible for their upbringing and not the other way around!

Children under school age need very clear boundaries with always a clear "yes" or "no." Arguments bring nothing at that stage and, if needed, the child can be swiftly removed from the state of arguing by clear action on the parent's part. Whether it is a time-out or some other method you use, you can find something that works effectively. That being said, younger children also need a hug and a cuddle pretty soon after being disciplined to be reassured of their parents' love. As children enter the elementary or grammar school stage, they need more of an explanation. However, they need to still know who is in authority. In the school stage, being very direct and purposeful in correction, without raising voices, helps children to know that they are loved, yet reinforces that there are boundaries to be respected. Kids at any stage will try to push a boundary, which is absolutely normal. However, when they know they are loved and totally accepted, they will begin to respect boundaries, understanding that they are for their own good.

Going back to unconditional love and acceptance, children need to be shown they are accepted just the way they are. It begins even in pregnancy. Doctors these days try to push for all kinds of tests to figure out whether a child is worthy of being brought into this world. When we do not take a strong stand against this kind of mentality and become advocates of our unborn child, we are already not accepting them unconditionally. A mother who can challenge a gynecologist, and say she will bring her child into this world no matter what the ultrasound shows, already gives a signal to the world about unconditional love and acceptance. I know of an amazing mom, from a ladies' Bible study group that I used to attend, whose love for her child, even unseen, is absolutely remarkable. She and her husband decided to bring their Down Syndrome child into this world, knowing very well that the baby would live outside the womb only a few hours. Hard as it was, they loved the baby in the womb, and outside the womb, before releasing him into Jesus' hands forever. What a beautiful testimony of Christian love to the hospital doctors, nurses, and indeed, the world around them.

Children blossom in an atmosphere where they feel that they belong, and as parents we need to make them feel like that at home. This means as parents we cannot be biased towards any child. Comparing siblings—constantly praising one and downplaying the other—is best avoided. Praising a child in whatever he or she can do, even if we cannot relate to that strength because it is not ours, is encouraging. By no means, should a child feel belittled or laughed at because of either a physical or a talent handicap. These things, even if done subconsciously most of the time, are often damaging for a child's soul and self esteem, and the shame he feels usually stays well into adult years. If a child is slow, let him be. He may not be the natural climber like his younger brother, but he may be a fast reader. Look for strengths in your child, not faults and handicaps. Moreover, if we want our kids to listen to us, we must model it by being good listeners ourselves. Do we take an active interest in what interests them, even if we are not naturally inclined towards those interests ourselves?

I am not suggesting that we need to be able to do or understand everything that they like, but we can show interest in their likes and passions, and we can be active listeners.

Knowing them well means we can guide them as to whether a particular passion is God-honoring and good for them, or not. According to my experience, there is definitely one thing we need to be able to show an interest in a child's life and passions...and that is time. Once again, both investment of our time as a mom into our children's lives plus a large dose of wisdom from the Lord are absolutely necessary to be able to show interest in our own children's lives. When time is short, we tend to get stressed by the smallest things, snappy at our kids for talking too much, and impatient when hearing about their day. Analyze one busy day in your life, as you interact with the kids, and see whether or not this is true for you too.

Keeping communication channels open is very important even for children under ten years. Working at communicating with little ones helps to continue that practice in preteen and teen years. It's best not to act totally shocked when your first grader comes home and talks in detail about how babies are made because she heard a few details in school. Or when your little guy uses a word that was never supposed make it into his vocabulary. My tip would be to breathe deep, go away for a moment to pray, asking God for a lot of wisdom.

Then come and talk to your child by first hearing him out fully. Best not to lecture him immediately about the evils of this world. He might think twice before telling you the next time. Or he may not want to shock you again and see that troubled look on your face.

We must pray for God's wisdom and the right words to use daily to handle sensitive situations. Our children should really feel free to come and talk to us. If at any point you feel like your son or daughter is closing up or feels the need to lie, take him or her out one-to-one and have a fun bonding time together. Give him or her the time to open up. Never stop praying, along with your husband, for raising your children. If you are married, please don't try to carry out this very challenging responsibility all by yourself. If you and your husband are not in agreement over parenting issues, I would encourage you again to tackle the causes of marital strife and find help in that area. If you are a single mom, perhaps you can find a godly woman as a prayer partner to support you.

Because God loves us He has "given us everything we need for living a godly life" (2 Peter 1:3). As parents, in the same way, we give our children all they need because we love them. Sally Clarkson in her book *The Mission of Motherhood* says that loving our children unconditionally means that we are committed to giving them what they need[14]. Notice there is a difference between what children need and what they want. Many a times we are tempted to show our unconditional love for our children by giving them what they *want*, which may not be the thing they *need* for their safety or development. A child who constantly whines and nags until mommy buys the candy bar at the store gets what he wants, his mother's attention and the candy, so he's encouraged to behave the same way the next time. If his mother does not succumb to his wishes the next time, he might start screaming and kicking and even threaten to run away. The mother, very self-conscious of disapproving glances from fellow shoppers, may decide to give her son again what he wants and this pattern continues. The child feels happy that he has demonstrated authority over his mother and mistakes it for his mother loving him no matter what. This same child, unless guided, may well go onto doing bigger mischief in his teenage and adult years always expecting his dear mummy to bail him out no matter what.

In contrast, a mother who gets her screaming toddler out of the stroller to tell her calmly, "No," but gives her attention by hugging her will teach both love and boundaries. Doing this takes more time and patience. If telling her calmly, yet with authority, that she will get a piece of chocolate when she has used the potty the next time, doesn't solve the problem, consider that she may be hungry and would benefit from a healthy snack. If after all this, she still does not calm down, then the mother hugs her more and distracts her by telling stories about different objects in the supermarket aisle. This way, the child's possible need for attention has been met by a big hug, and her hunger has been addressed. Sometimes, nothing will make her happy, short of getting just what she wants. Having said all this, I will be honest and tell you there have been times I have felt like completely flipping out, times when my three-year-old went on screaming, unwilling to hear me out in any way. Patience lost, yes. What did I gain later? I won the opportunity to repent and be calmer the next time. I praise God that He gives me extra chances and helps me to deal with my own impatience during my kids' disobedient moments.

I have noticed with each of my five children, as well as on several other children, that children thrive when boundaries are given to them. Christian psychologists and authors Dr. Henry Cloud and Dr. John Townsend in their popular book *Boundaries with Kids* say that when boundaries are clear, children develop a well-defined sense of who they are and what they are responsible for—the ability to choose, the understanding that if they choose well, things will go well and the other way around[15]. Kids that are left to figure out things for themselves can become very insecure and are bound to take out their frustration at not knowing how to act in some way or another.

I can't say we can blame the badly-behaved child in a restaurant who sends his spaghetti with meatballs flying across the room and is allowed to get away with that behavior. Sadly, many restaurants are not keen on serving families with kids, because apparently kids do not know how to behave in a restaurant. Can we really blame a child if he has never been shown how to eat properly or been given a consequence of some nature for his inappropriate behavior? For the very protective moms out there, please do note that correcting a bad behavior, or giving consequence to a child, does not have to involve shaming a child in front of others like spanking or yelling at him in a shop. Please do find out what works for you and your child before you lose your cool in the shop. I would encourage and urge you to take time to really get to know your child/ children and to learn how to motivate and teach them to become responsible and respectful individuals in society. As we guide our children with God's love, we give them a sense of security that will help them make good choices in life. Giving age-appropriate boundaries to children will not stifle them, but rather it will protect them. Nurture and protection are what we loving parents want to give our precious ones.

Creating memories

"What kind of childhood did you have?" In looking at the root causes for certain behaviors, this seems to be one of the most commonly asked questions by therapists or counselors of their adult clients. In my own experience as a counselor, I've heard clients explain that certain childhood experiences affect their parenting, marriages or friendships. Many childhood experiences are based on remembering events from the distant past or are based on the retelling of events by parents or relatives, or on viewing photographs. Because of the subjective nature of memory, these recollections may not always accurately reflect the quality of childhood times. However, children tend to store memories in the form of overall *impressions* of incidents and then remember these later on in life. Whether it is an exact memory or a perceived memory, research in psychology shows that both have an influence on psychological well-being during adulthood. Psychologist Dr. Krystine Batcho[16] reports, "Adults who believe they were cheated of the things, experiences, love, or acceptance that every child deserves can negatively impact relationships and feelings of adequacy and belonging." She goes on to say, "The impression of having had a happy childhood is associated with greater social connectedness, enhanced sense of self, and healthy behaviors. Adverse impressions of childhood are related to greater difficulty in relationships, self-insight, and dealing with distress."

What would constitute a happy childhood? Could it be mommy or daddy always being there? Or being able to pursue interests freely, such as dance, without being excessively pushed? Could it be specific events, such as camping under the stars, or general traditions, like going out for Sunday meals as a family? It might be a combination of several things such as parental togetherness, sharing fun times with siblings, going on roadtrips, or having the freedom to follow dreams. The instances that people remember as contributing to happy or sad experiences are filtered through the lens of childhood. Memories create the perception of one's childhood. And perception affects adult behavior, the sense of well-being, and the ability to withstand and cope with a variety of life situations. We, as parents, can give our children the gift of happy memories by purposefully creating those memories now.

The Doubts and The Desire

It feels like the last ten years have flown by with me being so busy with homemaking and mothering—baby care, cooking, cleaning, driving, laundry, and giving instructions— that I hardly have a moment to relax or even feel like doing fun stuff with the kids. My kids enjoy playing board games. Honestly, for me board games are more like "bored games," as they do not particularly excite me. Sometimes, I cannot concentrate because there's the toddler who is pulling on electrical cords...again! I am so thankful I have a husband who actually enjoys playing board games, so that as a family, we are able to create memories by playing board games, in spite of my dislike of them—what a relief!

To be honest, creating long lists of fun activities to do with kids isn't my greatest strength, but family fun is very important to the idea of creating lasting, positive childhood memories. Making this list has allowed me to experience the grace of God by showing me that no mom needs to know or do it all. God has been teaching me that my desire to see my children happy and nurtured is a good thing, and that He will honor that desire. There have also been times that He has reminded me to prioritize my activities, so I could focus on the important things. If getting in some time with my little ones, building Lego towers on the floor, means having a not-so-clean house, then so be it. If they have burgers and fries one evening instead of a healthy meal, and have a great time outside, then so be it. The joy of seeing them laugh, playing together and trying new things outweighs the need for following strict routines. You must know by now that I am a fan of routine, but I am more of a fan of making memories.

I have recently met quite a few moms who share their doubts about being a good mom. They feel inadequate in their ability to do stuff with their kids that will be fun. Many women suffer from post-partum depression, making it even harder to play with their older kids and they feel guilty about it. I have also struggled with the feeling that I am not doing "enough" with the kids. Sometimes, I have worried, *My kids are missing out on all the fun. I am not a good mom because I don't join them in the pool when they want or because I don't go on enthusiastic bike rides with them.* It has taken a lot of grace from the Lord to learn that I am still the mom that God has created for these specific children and that God is the one Who has created me, just the way I am.

God has also given me a husband who enjoys doing things with the kids that I do not necessarily enjoy. He even opened my eyes to see that there are plenty of things that I do with the kids that they *enjoy* which my husband does not even try doing. A husband and wife, working as a team, is indeed a good way of creating memories for kids. There are of course activities and events that we, as a whole family, like doing together. Every family needs to find out what those things are. You may be surprised at the simple things you can do as a family that bring great joy and laughter to the whole group.

In our case, it can be as simple as looking at family photos on a big screen and reminiscing. Although, there's a need to do stuff together with kids that brings them enjoyment, parents should avoid getting into the trap of trying to keep up with what everyone else is doing with their kids. The important lesson I have been learning in my mothering journey is that we should do the things that we actually enjoy doing. The kids will cherish and remember those ordinary times spent with mom, enjoying each other's company. Simple things like a walk in the park, jogging together, laughing at silly jokes, or going to out for ice cream all have the potential to create long lasting, happy memories.

My own mother could neither drive nor bike. Neither was she one bit interested in sports. She could not dance or speak different languages. There are many things that she could not actively do with me. However, she always took an active interest in what *I* liked doing and encouraged me in those activities. She was the one who spent hours taking me on the bus to dance class. She bought me expensive imported motor racing magazines because I was crazy about following Formula One racing—in those days motor-racing magazines were an absolute novelty where I grew up. My mother and I shared silly jokes and laughed like crazy. We enjoyed going to cafes and restaurants, just the two of us. How distinctly I remember the places we used to visit, even the smell and taste of those hot *naans* and creamy chocolate truffles!

Fun and Memorable Times

I ask my children from time to time what relaxes them, what gives them joy, and what kind of activities they like doing. I find this to be a very good unraveling/getting-to-know-your-kids exercise. It also helps me to know how I can best encourage them and bring them happiness. I might not be able to give them everything they want—like flying on a horse, or flying to their home country and coming back, in a day—but it does help me know who they are, what they desire, and what the world looks like to them. This also helps me to plan activities that meet their needs, in a realistic way! Family traditions and family fun times are usually things that a child carries onto adulthood as memories. Every tradition and activity planned by the family may not be what each child wants to do, but children do learn an important lesson here: to live together, looking out for the needs and interests of others, thus living out a biblical command and principle of humility (Philippians 2:4-5).

As a family, we love to have some traditions that we can call our own. I have to admit that in the busyness of life and social engagements, some things from time to time slip past us. And that is sad. For our family, each of us loves some kind of routine on special days. For example, Sunday is our family and church day, which means we consciously try to avoid taking on other engagements or activities. A Sunday tradition is going to church and then for a meal. The kids love going out to eat. We need to remind them regularly not to take these things for granted, since it's really a luxury to be able to go out for meals regularly. My husband and kids like playing board games on a Sunday. Although that is not really my thing, I do try to participate with them for the good of the group.

Family holidays usually create memories too, both good ones and bad ones! I remember our fun beach times in sunny Cape Town as much as I remember the non-stop throwing up of airsick kids on the plane! Yuck! The kids remember the fun of handshaking with the cute dolphins, as well as seeing the cheeky monkeys snatch food out of their hands. Driving through the Gotthard Tunnel in Switzerland, 16.9 km or 10.5 mile, gave my young kids such a thrilling experience that even years later my older ones remember it as "the fourth longest tunnel in the world". Travel is a great way to learn geography facts!

Apart from holidays, there may be many other occasions that make for happy childhood memories. Having eventful, creative birthday parties, without necessarily spending tons of money, is very special. As the children grow older, being able to explore the neighborhood with friends might create more memories. It's good to give kids some freedom and flexibility to explore with their friends, as long as we know where they are. Building sand castles, learning to ride a bike and to swim, toasting marshmallows over a bonfire, and dancing in the rain are just some of the things that parents can do with their kids to create fun and memorable childhood times.

Another important aspect of creating pleasant memories and emotional security is to spend one-on-one time with kids. If there is more than one child in your family, it's a good idea to have some quality, individual time with one child only. Your child will feel special and can express her desires and open her heart in a way that may not be possible when a sibling is around. These times are especially essential for certain periods such as, for example, after a new baby is born. Your older child will always appreciate some mommy or daddy away from home. Even if it is just a half-hour of playtime at the nearby park, try to give your full attention to the child without talking about the baby, unless your child brings up little baby into the conversation. One-on-one time means the child is not competing with a smartphone or with the baby at home and or the mountain of laundry awaiting you.

I have also experienced great joy in taking just one child out, even if only for an hour or two. We stop for a snack at a restaurant, or spend time at the playground, or even go window-shopping. It's important to do this when that child had been displaying signs of attention-seeking behavior such as arguing, being cranky, clingy or generally annoying. It makes such a difference when that child is removed from the usual environment and is transported to another world, where it is only he and his mommy. I usually come back home with a much happier child who has gotten the attention he needed, without having to fight for it among a crowd of people. Of course, having one-on-one time may not be possible on a regular basis, depending on your childcare situation. But if daddy leaves work early, or is home for the weekend, or if you have helpers like grandparents, friends, or a trusted babysitter, it can be a rewarding experience for both you and your children.

CHAPTER 5
INVESTING IN THEIR PHYSICAL DEVELOPMENT

For you created my inmost being; you knit
me together in my mother's womb.
— Psalm 139:13

We live in a world today that is flooded with choices for kids' activities, access to toys encouraging motor skills, and varieties of electronic/digital aids for encouraging physical development. Parents with spending power dispense thousands of dollars every year so their children will grow and develop to their full potential. Whether it is buying the healthiest milk formula on the market, or enrolling them in the premier ballet school, most parents have the "best" in mind when it comes to their child's overall physical development. It's a good thing that we have so many choices available so our children can move, be active, and grow up healthy. However, this is hardly a substitute for the love and attention that a child's body gets from its mama in the little years.

There's a reason why God has designed the mother and child's body the way He has. The mother houses the child from conception in her body and provides all the nourishment it needs to grow and be safe. When the time is right, the baby comes out and attaches itself firmly to the mother's body, which continues to provide a warm, cocooning environment. The close contact with her skin makes the baby feel safe and protected in spite of its new, strange, and bright environment. Keeping this original design in mind, we need to remind ourselves of the important role we play in our child's physical development.

As moms, the care for our children's bodies begins even from the time we become pregnant. The way we eat and take care of our pregnant bodies has a big effect on the growth of the baby. After the baby comes out, the mother continues to be the source of nourishment to baby—whether you are breastfeeding or giving formula, you are providing the building blocks for your baby's body. In the toddler years and beyond, you are responsible for taking care of what goes into your child's body by way of food and drink. And which mama does not want her baby to sleep at night? Enough rest and sleep are essential factors for a child's physical development, and it's part of the job of the mother to make sure they get enough sleep. A healthy body helps to maintain a healthy mind. Good sleep contributes to both increased mental concentration as well as to an overall happy disposition. Baby's good sleep also makes mom happy because she can get enough sleep too, and everyone else in the family feels it!

I must say right away: I am neither a trained nutritionist nor a physician. I am neither a professional health coach nor a baby sleep-trainer. However, becoming a mom to five children in eight years, gave me abundant opportunity for hands-on experience in all these areas. I am a researcher by nature, so having my first child led me to study for hours and hours on topics of healthy eating, lactation, dealing with common childhood illnesses or whatever other random issue came up.

All the information collected and practiced on the first child helped me with caring for my next ones. However, every new child lends itself to learning new things about children that you never previously thought of even reading about. Much of what you will read in the next few pages is based on my own personal experiences and what I've learned from mothering. I sincerely hope that what I share might help or encourage another mama. I would also like to say here that *what I share is not a specific formula, but rather some general principles that you may adapt to your own situation.* I would encourage you to pray about how you can apply those principles specifically for your child who is distinct and unique.

Caring for God's Beautiful Creation: The Pregnant Body

Before I share about investing in your child's physical development, I would like to point out the importance of taking care of yourself, and your baby, even before he says, "Hello!" to the world. Healthy habits developed during pregnancy are a good head start for your journey into motherhood. Before I was married, before the thought of having kids crossed my mind, I thought of pregnancy as a kind of a physical handicap. I pictured women lugging their big tummies around, wearing baggy clothes and looking generally tired. That was not a very attractive picture to me. When I became pregnant myself, I did not want to look big or wear baggy clothes, but I did not know what exactly lay ahead of me either. I wasn't sure of how to take care of a pregnant body and learned as I went.

I tried to strictly follow the nutrition advice given in well-known pregnancy books to keep my growing baby healthy, but I neglected the exercise part so I wasn't happy about how I looked and felt. From my second pregnancy on, I realized that I did not need to "eat for two." I needed to exercise, as long as the doctor thought it was advisable, in order to feel well myself and provide a good growing environment for my baby. Babies in the womb need a good level of blood flowing into their bodies and regular, not necessarily vigorous, exercise in pregnancy helps with blood circulation and releases good hormones called endorphins.[17]

So, what is eating right and healthy? Does one really need to eat for two? Am I allowed to eat certain kinds of food? These are very typical questions that any new pregnant woman is likely to ask. Thankfully, there are a variety of good books on the market that answer these questions. What I am giving you here are some principles of healthy eating while pregnant, which can be carried forward to the nursing period as well. I have summarized these from different sources as well as from my own (and of several friends') experiences.

Refine Your Diet, Even if You Are Already a Healthy Eater

Pregnancy calls for fine-tuning your eating, which does not mean that you are to eat radically different unless your current diet is really unhealthy. A few more calories from healthy food choices, adding more protein, taking vitamin supplements and avoiding certain foods might do the trick. Pregnant women do not need to eat for an extra person. After all, have you seen the size of those little ones in the womb? In fact, no extra calories are needed in the first and second trimesters, and only about 200 calories extra a day during the the third one[18]. Eating healthy extra calories is key. Lean sources of protein would be chicken, fish—salmon is a great choice—and red meat, which is a good source of iron. Protein from lentils and beans can be considered part of healthy pregnancy nutrition too. A well-rounded diet would include whole grains, dairy, vegetables and fruit. It's very important to wash all your veggies and fruit thoroughly, before consuming them, since pregnant women are more susceptible to certain food-borne illnesses.

Avoid Eating Certain Food and Drinks

Raw fish such as sushi and sashimi should be avoided during the whole of pregnancy as well as unpasteurized milk and soft cheeses such as Brie, Camembert, blue, and Gorgonzola[19].

Do ask at the cheese counter, or read the label carefully, to determine if the cheese is made of unpasteurized milk (mostly soft ones and some hard ones) and stay clear of these. However, not all soft cheeses are from unpasteurized milk and so it is still possible to enjoy a nice soft variety without being worried sick! Similarly, raw or undercooked meat or "cold-cured" meats such as salami, carpaccio and parma ham should be avoided. These food items can carry bacteria, which could potentially harm the unborn child.

There is no need to give up on your daily "cup of Joe", but it's probably best to cut down. Research shows that pregnant women consuming more than 200 mg of caffeinated drinks like coffee, tea, cola, hot chocolate are twice as likely to miscarry as those who do not consume such amounts.[20] I cut out caffeine completely in my first pregnancy, but did drink a cup of coffee almost every day in my subsequent pregnancies with no huge difference in the way I felt in the pregnancies or in the way the babies turned out! Drinking alcohol is an absolute no-no because exposing the fetus to it can lead to physical, mental and emotional defects in the baby[21].

Start Taking Prenatal Vitamin Supplements

A good, healthy diet is extremely important, but sometimes it's just not enough for your growing baby. Certain prenatal vitamin supplements are essential in ensuring the proper growth of the baby in the womb. Proper levels of folic acid is an absolute must, as I have been reminded by five different doctors in two countries. Lack of using this supplement has been linked to neural tube defects in babies such as spina-bifida.

My very first pregnancy ended in miscarriage. I never knew the reason, except that it was God's will, and I accepted this after a good deal of questioning and struggling with God's decision. I'm not implying anything important here, but looking back, my diet those days was rather poor and I had absolutely no information on what healthy eating during pregnancy involved. However, a few months before I became pregnant with my first child, God brought some new friends into my life when my husband and I moved to a new city. These friends were seasoned moms and they shared some treasures of knowledge with me. I am so thankful for the friend who told me that I should start taking folic acid supplements even before I was pregnant to prepare my body to carry another life!

Eat Frequent, Smaller Meals

In my first pregnancy, I suffered the consequence of eating heavy, full meals and how! Full-size meals can increase unpleasantness like nausea and vomiting in the early part of pregnancy and heartburn, indigestion and bloating in the later part. It's better to eat five or six smaller portions, throughout the day, including healthy snacks in between like nuts, seeds, and cheese. As the baby grows inside, it tends to crowd the stomach and other organs, making it more difficult for food to pass through the digestive tract, as it normally would. If you have morning sickness, eating crackers and hard cookies can ease the nausea, which can be worse when you're hungry. Always be mindful of portions and avoid foods that are loaded with sugar or are very fatty because they are not necessarily healthy to eat, may cause weight gain, and can contribute to nausea. Why make matters worse?

Move, Mama, Move

As long as the pregnancy is in the medical sense, and a green light has been given by the doctor, moderate exercise is a very beneficial during pregnancy. This is not the time to hide indoors, tucked comfortably under your blankie, enjoying hot chocolate! Save such things for rainy or snowy days. Some form of moderate physical exercise is good for both mom and baby. The tiny one gets plenty of oxygen and good levels of blood circulation and the mama gets better sleep, better digestion, manageable weight gain, less bloating and swelling, and even a lovely glow on her skin. I found walking to be the best exercise for me during pregnancy. Barring extreme weather conditions or days when you don't feel well (listen to your body), there's no reason why walking cannot be done. A half an hour walk, at a moderate to brisk pace, is an excellent way to remain fit and keep weight gain under control. Swimming and pre-natal Pilates are also good activities. If your fitness level is very good before you started your pregnancy, light jogging, dancing, and light aerobics are also advisable. However, it is potentially dangerous to engage into contact sports such as tennis, soccer, or martial arts where injury and collision are possible[22].

I remember in my first pregnancy, I used to lie down at the slightest instance of dizziness or nausea. I only walked to get my daily groceries and other necessities, but was not conscious about walking regularly. Low activity levels, coupled with too much food in the name of "good nutrition", caused me to gain quite a few extra pounds, especially towards the end of my pregnancy. The added weight made any movement in the last few weeks even more difficult! In contrast, in the four subsequent pregnancies, I was very active and took the time to consciously exercise, which made me fit and healthy right up to birth. Staying fit helped me be able to climb seven floors right up to the start of labor with my third child and manage a big overseas move with four little kids and a bump! Walking was especially helpful and seemed to battle nausea, bloating, and that weight gain. Keep in mind that some weight gain will automatically happen due to baby's growth, increased water, blood, heavier breasts etc.

I have some good news for you if you are reading this book and thinking "Oh dear, I had such a heavy pregnancy and did not enjoy those months," but would like to have more children in the future. It is possible to enjoy a good pregnancy and feel great. No matter whether you are pregnant for the first or the fifth time, every pregnancy can be a different experience. In spite of morning sickness, heartburn, sleeplessness and other typical issues, carrying a child can be a joyful time, if you choose to make it that way. Yes, a lot of our pregnancy experience depends on our own attitude and self-discipline.

Our baby is here!! Yay! Now What?

There is hardly anyone who will disagree with this: a newborn baby needs a lot of time and care! A tiny baby does need pretty much round-the-clock attention because of feedings, diaper changes, and crying for reasons unknown to us. If you think about it, it's really quite amazing that moms somehow manage to get through the newborn stage, with such sleepless nights and frazzled nerves. I think the only way to explain is this: that God gives and He provides. Taking care of babies, tiny tots, toddlers, preschoolers and school-age children, I have learned a few lessons that I would like to share with you. Perhaps you will find something that works for you and allow you to get some much-needed sleep. Again, what I will share here is broad principles, not formulas or short cuts. Every human is unique and we must not forget that raising one takes wisdom from above and precious time.

Feeding Baby

You must have read or heard this often, and I will only reinforce it: if you are able to, then please breastfeed and do not give up because it might be hard in the beginning. Unless you are absolutely not able due to some physical impossibility, occurring on the side of either mother or baby, try giving your baby only breast milk for the first six months. Mother's milk is designed to provide the baby all it needs for growth and health. Though you might worry about whether the baby is getting enough milk, as opposed to formula, where you can see exactly how much the baby is drinking, don't be discouraged by this. I was tempted to give up on nursing my first baby after a couple of weeks because it was so physically tiring and it seemed like the baby kept falling asleep rather than drinking! But I am so glad I did not give up.

Breast-feeding is simpler than many new moms realize and, for me, it got easier with each baby. The milk is always there and there is never a need to sterilize bottles or take the time to warm up milk, especially middle of the night. Sadly, I could not nurse my youngest child, who was born with a cleft palate, which made breastfeeding impossible. Sterilizing bottles made this post-baby phase the most difficult among all my children!

Another thing concerning feeding babies is that, after the first three to four weeks following birth, baby can be put on a feeding schedule. For me, this method has always worked. There was never an issue with the baby being hungry, and it seemed that an increase in security emerged from the routine feedings. The baby knew he would get his milk, so there was no need to start screaming in hunger. The little tummy got used to it. I have seen some first time mums—and that was me too—trying to feed the baby whenever it cried! I don't know whether this instinct is out of sheer panic or from following traditions or trends. You might hear your grandma saying, "Feed that crying baby. She must be hungry," and you obediently follow her advice. However, it does not really help the baby to be fed when what he really wants might be to release gas or to tell you that he has had quite enough milk. I found it easiest to put the baby on a three-hour feeding pattern, except at nighttime, when the time gaps would be slowly increased to create a sleeping habit. I will talk about sleeping in more detail soon, but first let me share a few pointers about developing healthy eating habits for growing children.

Nutrition for Your Growing Child

It goes beyond saying that healthy eating is absolutely essential for growing children. This does not mean cutting out all fun, delicious foods and eating only steamed vegetables and broiled fish. No, developing healthy eating habits for the whole family, does not mean eating tasteless, bland food. In addition, preparing these kinds of meals doesn't have to be overwhelming. There are so many good food blogs with amazing, and free, recipes for all types of diet requirements and restrictions. Eating whole grains, including generous portions of fruits and veggies daily, choosing healthy oils for cooking, and keeping fast-food visits to a minimum are simple ways of making sure that kids get a balanced nutrition in their growing bodies. Listed below are a few of my favorite food blogs, which I check out from time to time. I hope these will give you plenty of ideas for being creative in the kitchen and feeding healthy meals to family and friends:

- www.raisehealthyeaters.com
- www.wellnessmama.com
- www.superhealthykids.com
- www.naturallyella.com

- www.bbcgoodfood.com
- www.smittenkitchen.com
- www.anjumanand.co.uk (for healthy Indian meals, to add some exotic flavor to your family meals)
- www.thebettermom.com (check out the section on recipe and meal planning)

Too much sugar is not good because it makes most kids hyperactive and restless (I have observed that in many kids). Excess sugar in the diet may also make them vulnerable to developing potential illnesses later on in life, such as diabetes. My personal guidelines in this area are simple. Be careful of feeding kids breakfast cereals on a regular basis, since they are often loaded with sugars; it's better to always check the packaging and choose the varieties that have no added sugar. Unless your child has been diagnosed with specific allergies or skin problems, there may not be a need to completely cut out all cookies and cakes. However, allowing these treats to be enjoyed from time to time, instead of every day, can also motivate healthy eating as they begin to look at some of their healthy foods as treats. We live in a world now with so many healthy meal choices available in restaurants and grocery stores—gluten free, dairy free, low fat—good nutrition is right at out fingertips. It's beyond the scope of this book to dig deeper on the topic of nutrition, but I would strongly encourage you to look online, or in your local bookstores for books on healthy kids and family recipes, together with the blogs mentioned above. It's easy to neglect a well-balanced, healthy-eating lifestyle for your kids when you're swamped with many different activities. When time is scarce, keep it simple. But keep it healthy.

Sleeping

Once again, I wish there was a magic formula for babies sleeping through the night or having a good sleep routine during the day, but I doubt there is a one-of-a-kind formula that will suit every baby. However, as long as baby is healthy and well, there are some basic principles of sleeping that can be applied. These principles could be helpful for setting a good sleeping routine. My caveat: much of what I am saying here is from my own experience and you are welcome to disagree. However, all five of my kids have started sleeping through the night pretty early on—from about two months of age. I understand that every family, every parent, every child is different and that is why I am not suggesting you follow my method to the letter. Perhaps you can take something from these principles and apply it to your particular family situation?

- Begin with Prayer: Prayer to God—asking for His help and wisdom, as well as listening to Him—is the starting point of training your baby to sleep. It's necessary to acknowledge that, without God's help, nothing can be achieved. When I say strict formulas don't work, I mean it. We need to seek God's wisdom, individually, for each child to learn the best way to do sleep training with her. Whenever you face frustration, and feel you cannot take it anymore, go to God on your knees and cry out for His help, just as the Psalmists did (e.g. Psalm 40:1,2).

- Give Consistent Physical Touch and Closeness: If a baby gets enough cuddles and physical attention throughout the day, her tank will be full and she will cry less for physical touch at night. Even if you have to care for other children, try to keep your baby close to you whenever possible. The mother's touch, as well as her voice, is reassuring to the little one. Having said that, I am not really a fan of my children sharing the bed with me. Two reasons: I want my marriage bed to be the marriage bed. And, the child and parents both get more oxygen and therefore, better sleep.

• Enough Downtime: This principle can be applied in various childhood stages in different forms. With a newborn baby, from birth until about seven to eight weeks, I have found it very helpful to give the baby some "alone time" away from the general hustle and bustle of the busy family or a busy routine. If there are many siblings around or you are likely to be around other people most of the day, it would be wise not to expose the baby to everyone, all the time. This is because babies experience and process everything that goes on around them, so they tend to carry their "stress" with them until it comes out later, usually in the evening. Even as babies grow into toddlers and preschool years, this downtime is very important. I have found that, during each day, at least one nap and some quite moments of free play or looking at a book, are very important to sleeping peacefully later at night.

- A Regular Routine: There is a saying that humans are slaves to habit. I don't know how much of this is true for adults, but for children the saying applies. Children respond well to routines, gaining security from repeated, familiar, and predictable schedules. I have found that a routine of established feeding times, a bath, and dressing in jammies, helps babies to understand the concept of "bed time". Trying any bed-time routine before six weeks of age might be a futile exercise, as babies' feedings are frequent and they are unable to distinguish between night and day. However, from about seven weeks on, it is possible to start working toward a routine with the baby. The non-negotiables for my babies were feeding every three to four hours throughout the day and a longer evening feed, followed by a bath and changing for bed. Another must for me was praying while nursing at bedtime, just before putting the baby into her crib for the night. I prayed that God would protect her and watch over her. When I left the room, these prayers reminded me that our little princess was safe in the hands of the Creator of the whole universe, the Sovereign Lord. What better assurance can there be? As children grow older, it is good to continue the routine of regular nap/downtimes and an established bedtime routine of bath, praying, cuddling, and reading books together. These habits help children to sleep more peacefully, but also give them added emotional security.

• Beware of Exposures: Once something is seen, it cannot be unseen. As parents, we must be very intentional about what we allow our children watch, or hear, from the time they are very young. If we expose our babies to too much noise, activity or the colorful flickering pictures on television, they are bound to react. Babies become more restless, the more things they are exposed to, especially in terms of colorful and noisy media. I am speaking from my experience and observation. If they were exposed to sensory experiences that were not good for them, our babies and older children tended to have restless sleep or have nightmares. I am always surprised when I hear of three or four-year-olds being allowed to watch TV shows or movies with mature content. Nowadays, even children's movies depict violence, conflict, alien characters (that look scary), excessive action, and subtle sexual themes. While teenagers and adults are equipped to process these situations and characters in a manageable way, a younger child may not be able to, which can lead to distress. Children react to this kind of mature material in a different way, so there is good reason for age appropriate film certifications (for example, PG, G, Adult, Mature Content etc.).[23] Hear what the Psalmist, David, says in Psalm 101:2-3:

> "I will conduct the affairs of my house with a blameless heart.
>
> I will not look with approval on anything that is vile."

- How Much "Crying it Out" Is Too Much? I know there are several theories about this. Some sleep gurus advocate absolutely no crying for babies when they are falling asleep. And then there are experts who advise you to let your baby "cry it out" for as long as needed, until he learns to falls asleep alone. This is confusing. On the one hand, it feels heartless to ignore the cries, yet on the other, all of that crying feels sure to drive you nuts! What's a mama to do?

The first thing would be to ask God for wisdom about how long to let the baby cry in the crib, or whether to let him cry at all. For each set of parents this answer may be different.

o For me, I knew I needed my sleep in order to be ready and able to care for the baby and other children during daytime. And therefore, I did not mind if my older baby cried for some time, provided it was not usually more than five minutes at a time. In the immediate weeks after baby's birth, I did not really let him cry out unless I desperately needed to shower or go to the bathroom. Holding and cuddling are important aspects to make the newborn feel safe and comforted. After about six or seven weeks, I started to let her cry a bit. After a feeding or rocking her, when I transferred the sleeping baby from my arm to her crib, she would cry. Sometimes more, sometimes less. However, I usually did not let her cry for longer than five to seven minutes and, at that point, I would always pick her up, give her a cuddle, rock her, sing to her, and put her back to the crib. Such a routine usually would go on for about an hour, for a few days. This is a key stage that requires a lot of prayer, patience, perseverance, and determination, as well as a little bit of a tough heart! This is the "make or break" stage. From my experience, I can say that if you are able to persevere through this routine, then you might just have a sleeper in your family for the rest of the childhood years.

○ Important: I would not advise anyone to let a sick child cry for any length of time. Sick children need a lot of physical touch and care, and this is where a mother's sacrificial heart can be given a full test! Because we need added strength for times of illness, we should persevere in creating good sleeping habits, because a sleep routine allows mom and dad to sleep and remain energized to serve.

• Physical Activity: Sometimes we find it hard to invest the necessary time to ensure that our kids are getting enough exercise and outdoor playtime. We have a busy evening routine with Daddy rushing home from work, Mommy cooking, and the kids being put to bed. There are also piles of laundry to do during the day along with regular housework. Living up to these responsibilities may leave us feeling completely out of whack! However, if we learn to prioritize tasks, keeping the not-so-urgent activities to a minimum, then we may find our days becoming less stressful. As a result, we gain more time and energy that can be invested in taking the kids to the park to play, or just go out for a walk. Fresh air and enough physical movement are very important for children's growth. Moreover, physical activity promotes better sleeping.

○ For babies under one year, I would encourage you to practice age-appropriate activities in order to check their gross and fine motor skill development. Your pediatrician will be able to inform you of the month-by-month developmental milestones you should be looking out for. Don't get nervous if your child is not doing everything that he or she is supposed to be doing at a particular stage, but if a developmental delay is more than a couple of months, it might be worthwhile getting things checked. For toddlers and preschoolers, plenty of fresh air and playtime outdoors should be included in the daily routine.

o When children reach school age, it's good to encourage them to participate in at least one physical activity on a regular basis—dancing, football, tennis, swimming, or skating —the choices are many these days. However, it's best not to overwhelm a child with too many activities, but rather encourage him or her to take on one or two enjoyable activities. You are their mom and they need your encouragement and motivation. But please do not overtire them! Too many activities will swamp them and affect their overall well-being and sleep.

I hope that this chapter and the previous one, help you to appreciate how caring for a child emotionally and physically is no trivial matter. Doing so requires a lot of effort and time on our part and, more importantly, guidance and help from above. God gives us precious children to look after them well. They are not short-term projects that we can squeeze in, in between our "main" jobs. We are accountable to their Creator for their well-being.

CHAPTER 6
WHAT ABOUT ME?

But seek first his kingdom and his righteousness,
and all these things will be given to you as well.
— *Matthew 6:33*

This book focuses on investing in our children, but in order to invest in them, we cannot neglect our own well-being. How we are investing in ourselves, so that we are better equipped to serve those that are around us? It might be a surprise to some of you to hear that it is absolutely okay to go out and enjoy a spa afternoon, get your nails done, or go out on a romantic date. Sometimes you need to do something for yourself in order to be refreshed and rejuvenated, so you can care for others

I was daydreaming one afternoon with a tall glass of latte and a piece of chocolate cake about how life would be if I did not have little ones to care for. I could have a high profile job wearing nice suits and using my analytical brain. Or I could go for long weekends away with *only* my husband—*just the two* of us, drinking champagne, and waking up late. I could travel the world over, visiting my long lost friends. I could go to the movies, eat out, do Pilates, run everyday, or meet friends for lunch dates without looking at my watch. My lifestyle could be upscale and carefree. I must have then dozed off at some point while dreaming, but I was suddenly awoken by cries of my two little ones. They reminded me very clearly that they wanted to be rescued from their cribs and set free for an afternoon of fun and playtime. Quickly, I was brought back to my real life. I rushed to get little ones out of their cribs, quickly giving them a snack, and then I scooted out to pick up the older kids from school. Sitting behind the steering wheel, I started thinking about my daydream from earlier. I thought of how boring my life would be if I did not have those cute little pests around! Yes, they may require a lot of work, physically and mentally, but my kids are a huge blessing. They are carrying on the family name and will be great company in old age, but more importantly, I get to know God deeper through them.

I don't think God uses any better tool for "spiritual pruning" than to grow us through parenting. God has shown me the essence of sacrificial love through caring for my children. Parenting has helped me to better understand God's love for me, through Jesus. He has also exposed the filthy things inside of me that need thorough cleansing as part of my sanctification process. He has revealed hidden anger, impatience, and selfishness that I never knew existed in me. In my experience, though motherhood is a demanding job, it has immense spiritual benefits, and for that alone I am very thankful. I am glad that that God did not let me have that high-profile, swanky career and lifestyle.

Though I am filled with gratitude at the opportunity to be a mother, I must admit that there are times I wish I could get away for a bit to do things that I enjoy, without the kids. Is there anything wrong in thinking this way? I don't think so, because we all need time on our own to recharge our batteries. Otherwise we're running on empty and, before we know, we'll burn out. If you're like me, and have thought of taking some time off, but don't know how to do so, or feel guilty about leaving your kids, then do read on.

Before turning our attention to caring for ourselves, I would like to point out something I consider pertinent. The point of taking time out for us should not come from selfish motives; rather it should be done with the end goal of becoming better mothers. It isn't a natural *right* to have a manicure or to go out for a treat, but these activities are not wrong, and can be beneficial, if time allows and possibilities arise. However, having a mindset of putting my desires first, before the needs of my little ones are met, is perhaps a debatable one. If I am giving priority to my fitness routine, wellness/beauty regimen, or hobby class over meeting the spiritual, emotional and physical needs of my kids, then I might need to examine my lifestyle. As believers and followers of Jesus Christ, we are called to lay down our lives for Him and carry out the tasks *He* has given us to do. So, if we are chosen and called to be mothers, then we must acknowledge that this high calling comes from Him. We must do everything within our power to carry out this ministry well, with God's strength. "Everything" may include recharging and tanking up in different ways so that we are still able to reach out to the people we have been called to serve and disciple. Recharging and re-fuelling, however, needs to happen in God's time, according to the opportunities *He* provides. Therefore, the attitudes and actions of self-care need to be put into God's hands and be led by Him rather than by our own thinking.

I journeyed as a mother, with little or no outside help, for the first eight years of raising my kids. My husband and I took care of our kids, with no immediate family around. But praise God for all His provisions in dire times of need. We have always had good friends from church who were there, taking care of us, providing meals after childbirth, or taking care of older kids during the birth. Many helped with grocery shopping when I was down with the flu and could not get up to look after anything. Now, God has brought us to a different country, where it is very "normal" to have live-in household help and I am grateful for that privilege. God has allowed me the opportunity to take care of myself more regularly even though I have more children to care for. I am thankful for the different kinds of help He has always provided in different seasons.

Motherhood allows us to lay down our lives, as Christ has done for us (1 John 3:16). Yet, laying down our lives for God does not mean that those lives must become miserable, empty, and dull. On the contrary, God richly provides us with "everything for our enjoyment" (1 Timothy 6:17). He has created each of us in a different way, and He alone knows what is good for us to enjoy, and what we will be able to handle. For some women, enjoyment could be going hiking outdoors, in the fresh air. For another, relaxing might mean chilling by the pool with no worries and good book. To another mom, downtime may be going shopping alone, trying on clothes with no little people underfoot. The Bible says God cares for us, and He will give us what we need, when we need it (1 Peter 5:7). Our responsibility is to guard our hearts and motives, to make sure we keep our priorities in good order.

Spiritual Health

As we discuss taking care of ourselves, we must note that the spiritual condition of our hearts needs more looking after than anything else. Nurturing our spirits ensures that we won't lose focus or get sidetracked from what God has designed us to do. We should follow the pattern of how Jesus cares, rather than the pattern of this world. Remember, in Chapter 1, I talked about investing in our relationship with the Lord? What happens when we do that? *The outcome is a renewed mind and obedient heart that wants to do God's will.* This chapter is the outpouring of things I have learned as a result of investing in my own relationship with the Lord. As I mentioned before, parenting is a process of spiritual pruning because it teaches me more about God and His love.

Spending time with God, in the midst of parenting, allows me to develop a better understanding of the ministry of obedience and sacrificial love as modeled by God's own Son, Jesus. Here are three Scripture passages that we can learn from, to help us follow the example of Jesus Christ in obedience and sacrificial love:

Look at Hebrews 12:1-3:

And let us run with perseverance the race marked out for us, fixing our eyes on Jesus, the pioneer and perfecter of faith. For the joy set before him he endured the cross, scorning its shame, and sat down at the right hand of the throne of God. Consider him who endured such opposition from sinners, so that you will not grow weary and lose heart.

Motherhood can be considered to be one long race! It's hard, and we may often get tempted to become weary and lose heart. There are sleepless nights with children who are whining and complaining. There are injuries, sicknesses, and times of other people telling us what to do. Difficulties during mothering remind us of why it's so important to fix our eyes on Jesus, who took up His cross, and went through all the shame and disgrace associated with the cross. For what? "He endured the cross for the joy that was set before him" (v. 2). What is His joy? It's us! Our salvation, sanctification, and glory at being united with Him forever, bring Jesus joy. Likewise, I am to take up my cross and endure, with joy, all that comes along with being a mom who invests her all in her kids. We may endure the scorn of being considered foolish for opposing cultural norms by "giving up everything" for the sake of raising children. However, if I keep Jesus before me at all times, He will give me the courage to face this scorn. For what? For the joy set before me, the joy of seeing my kids walk with Jesus, in obedience to him.

Take a moment right now and read John 7:1-18; John 8:1-30.

- "Jesus told them, 'My time is not yet here; for you any time will do'" (John 7:6).

- "I always do what pleases him" (John 8:29).

These verses teach us a lot about doing things in the right time, doing everything in God's timing and approval.

Motherhood is comprised of different seasons. Some are more hands-on and intense, whereas others may allow us more time by ourselves, when the kids are in school. We need to give each season of motherhood, with all its challenges, joys and sorrows, to God and be eager do His will. There is a time and place for everything. Not every season will allow us to do the things that we want or are naturally talented in doing.

I love speaking in public. Before I had children, I used to do that regularly. Even having three kids, I could speak regularly in front of many people, lead ministries and teach at ladies' Bible studies. However, after I became pregnant with my fourth child, things changed. I gave up my public speaking ministry because I felt God was asking me to invest whatever energy I had at my home, the place of my most important ministry. I often itch to speak or teach, but I know now is not the time to do things the way I did before. God may give me opportunities to speak before a large audience later on, but right now I am in a different season. It doesn't mean I can't speak or teach. God is using those very gifts in a different way. When Jesus says, "For you any time is right" (John 7:6), I think of how we as moms and women tend to do things just because everyone else is doing it. Instead, we must enjoy the freedom we have of doing things in His timing.

Read John 10:11-18.

- "I am the good shepherd. The good shepherd lays down his life for the sheep" (vs. 11).
- "I lay it down on my own accord" (vs. 18).

As moms, we are called to be the shepherds of our children. Just as the good shepherd lay down his life, of his own accord, for his sheep, I am called to sacrifice my life for the sake of my children, for the benefit of them knowing Christ and His love. I make this sacrifice, voluntarily, in obedience to God's call on my life. I need to live my own life as God wants me to live, and be enslaved neither to the ideas of this world nor to the opinions of other Christians. However, giving up other things in life in order to be with kids does not mean doing everything for them. Children need more attention and supervision when they are little but as they grow older, we must guide them step-by-step to independence. In the baby and toddler stage, kids need lots of physical attention and touch. As they grow into more independent years from preschool to school, and beyond, the need to be constantly *with them* reduces. But our need to be there for them never changes.

As Christ's followers, our attitude and our willingness to put others first will always be tested. Motherhood is just one area that offers itself up as a daily challenge, as well as opportunity to practice faith and obedience. Some days I struggle when I think everyone else around me seems to have it altogether. However, the verses above are able to remind me of Whom I am following, and of what His nature is like. Fixing my eyes on Jesus is the only way I can stay focused on my calling, my God-given purpose, rather than being influenced by what other people say or do.

I hope these three Bible passages have illustrated the importance of caring for the spiritual condition of your heart, before you attempt to take care of your emotional and physical condition. Having examined the spiritual, how can we take care of ourselves in other ways so we can joyfully serve in this great ministry called motherhood? The following ideas have worked for me, as well as for many other wise women of God who come from different backgrounds, races, ages and nations.

The Mom-Care Toolkit for Women in Ministry to their Kids

We need to rest, take care of ourselves. We need time to remember that we are women, and wives as well, not just mothers. A well-rested mom will have more energy and patience for her whole family. Friend, you must:

- Invest in your relationship with God. As we have discussed, take time out regularly to nurture the most important relationship of all. This will give you strength for the day, guidance and wisdom for raising children and help you feeling refreshed in every way.

- Have fun times with your husband. Don't let the romance slip away from your marriage. What made you fall in love with your guy? Try to get help from trusted babysitters, friends or family and make it a habit to spend quality time with your man. Be it going out dining, doing an activity together, or simply laughing at each others' jokes, a solid marriage helps in not only raising happy kids, but keeps you feeling alive and beautiful as a woman.

- Get in touch with your creative side. Nurturing your creative side will help to feel refreshed. I don't mean that you have to paint like Picasso or sculpt like Michelangelo, but you can use your creative brain and hands. Some popular choices are knitting, quilting, scrapbooking, painting, painting or throwing pottery, playing a musical instrument, writing, learning a language, cooking and baking. I am someone who does not get any enjoyment out of sewing, knitting, or quilting. But I do like painting, when I have time. I also find cooking to be a huge creative outlet. But most of all, I like acting; I feel so alive when I am able to do it. Time may not always be on your side, but that is only partly true. Where there is a will there is a way. I encourage you to make it a priority to do what makes you come alive instead of thinking that your life is over once you are a mom!

- Take time out to do nothing but relax. Okay, this is really preaching to myself, but I write about what I need too. It's difficult for me to just sit down and relax and read a book when my to-do list is running around in my head. I love to just drink a hot coffee or tea and do nothing—with no distractions from smartphones or tablets—just enjoying the pure delight of a good cup of the strong, black, therapeutic liquid. This is a good exercise to keep turning things over to God and resting in Him. If you have someone to watch the kids, it is also great to get out and enjoy some time getting your nails done or having a spa day, if you enjoy that kind of stuff.

• Make exercise a part of your regular routine. Staying physically fit is a great habit. Running regularly not only helps me to stay in shape, but also keeps my mind much more alert and happy. Exercising releases chemicals in the body known as endorphins, and these are said to trigger positive feelings inside you. Regular exercise helps to maintain healthy weight, reduce stress, decrease depression, and lower the risk of heart-related illnesses, as well as diabetes. Do you have an exercise routine? Is there any physical activity you like or could think of taking up? Almost every city these days has Pilates, dance, or aerobic classes. And if not, it certainly has walkways!

• Don't be a frump! Eat well, dress well, and generally make an effort to look nice. Please don't get me wrong. Looking nice has nothing to do with what others say about you or having the latest fashion items. It has to do with you looking good for yourself and for your husband. Dressing in what looks nice to you, and to your husband, and in clothes that make you feel comfortable is key. Our worth should not come from outer things such as fancy clothes, jewelry, and hair but rather from the purity within (1 Peter 3:3,4). However, hanging around in baggy clothes and being generally unkempt does not give us much of a self-confidence boost either. The Proverbs 31 Woman, who is given as the example of a godly woman in the Bible, was also well-dressed (Proverbs 31:22).

- Get out of the house. Walking in the fresh air with your baby in a stroller is wonderful. But going out on your own, from time to time, is also very important. Go out to lunch with your friends. Experience the culture your city has to offer and broaden your horizons. For example, I love to go to classical music concerts or ballets. Are you a culture vulture? Or are you more the coffee and foodie type? Go out on your own or gather a group to go out with. Maybe there is a ministry in church that you can become involved so you can get out and be in fellowship others.

Motherhood is a high calling, which is to be fulfilled with the strength God provides. It is however, neither an end to your personal identity, nor should it be the only thing that gives you identity. You are you. You have been created by God with all the qualities, talents and gifts that are unique to *you.* Motherhood may be your calling, even the most important one. Your identity, however, comes from who you are in Christ. When you are a believer, your faith in Jesus Christ should define who you are. As a child of God, out of that identity, comes your purpose and calling.

If you do not take the moments of rest that are given and make the most of your opportunities for resting and regaining strength, then you will be at risk for, not only running empty, but for growing bitter in the long run. Many women blame their children later on in life for "ruining" their lives. They wished they had done something more useful with their lives. I encourage you to rest and have a well-balanced life, so that you can receive joy from serving in the ministry of motherhood.

CONCLUSION

I have poured out my heart to you concerning the importance of spending time with our precious little ones. A few years ago, as I was walking in the park with my children, I saw quite a few other ladies out with their babies in stroller or walking with their toddlers. As we stopped at the playground to play, I noticed something interesting. There were blonde kids with dark-skinned moms or kids and moms with no resemblance to each other at all. Having chatted with a few of the ladies at the playground, I realized that these ladies were not the kids' moms, but rather their "day mom" or nanny. I felt a little lost being the only mom actually out with my own children! For some, this is common: real mothers feeling more and more alienated when they choose to be with their own children. What a twisting of the original design of God who created mothers and children to be together! Even if this may be today's norm, I would encourage you and remind myself, to go back to God's Word, which says, "Do not conform to the pattern of this world" (Romans 12:2).

Many a mother feels overwhelmed at the thought of raising kids. To be honest, it is nothing unusual to think that way because it is indeed a big responsibility. After all, we are responsible for another human being's life! We often try to pass on the responsibility for raising our child to others, from a very young age, simply because we have determined in our minds that we cannot do it. Of course, we should rely on help whenever we can get it. We should not fall into the "super mama" trap, thinking we can, and must, do it all. But expecting nannies, daycare workers, teachers, or coaches to equip our children for adulthood undermines God's plan in making us their mothers.

Our little ones are placed in our care for a period of time, so that we can nurse them, nurture them, and train them up to be followers of Christ and respectful human beings. One day the little ones will grow up and leave the nest. We will not have much control over their comings and goings. However, the time we invest into their growth, especially spiritual, will bear fruit in later years because our God is faithful. He listens to the prayer of a faithful mother and honors her desire, *and consequently the time she has invested*, to see her children walking in the truth.

You are the mother of your children. You and I will not be perfect mothers. But we can give our best and leave the rest to our God, Who *is* perfect. Since God does not make mistakes, please don't doubt, even on days when you're overwhelmed, that you should not have been the mom to your kids, or a mom at all. On the contrary, you are the very mom God created for your children. You have all the characteristics and peculiarities that are unique to you. Today, commit to giving your motherhood journey to the Lord, with all its joys, sorrows, hopes, challenges and desires. Commit yourself, your husband and your children to the Lord every single day. Even if you think you've totally messed it up, remember into Whose hands you are committing yourself. He is able to make good from all the past moments of anger, yelling, poor choices, and whatever that you're not happy about since your mothering journey started. Give yourself once again to the Lord today and be determined in your heart to follow His instruction in mothering your children.

I hope you have gained some new insight from this book as I have talked about the different aspects of investing in our children. Let me recap. In Chapter One, I spoke about the importance of developing a habit of spending time with the Lord in order to know Him and His heart for motherhood. When we invest in this primary relationship, we can invest time and energy into our children. In Chapter Two and Three, I shared about how we can encourage the spiritual development of our little ones by (a) prayer, (b) knowing God through reading Scripture and talking about God, and (c) training in righteousness and disciplining. As investing time into the overall emotional well-being of our children is so important, I have devoted a whole chapter, Chapter Four, to this topic. Scripture as well as psychological research has shown the importance of good attachment relationship between a mother and her child. The role of family and marital unity, unconditional love and giving boundaries, as well as creating memories in childhood are building blocks of emotional security. Chapter Five demonstrated the importance of investing in the physical development of a child, starting even at the pregnancy stage. Nutrition, sleep, and physical activity are areas where we mothers are called to invest time. Last but not the least, in Chapter Six, I shared about how taking care of ourselves recharges us, so that we can devote ourselves to the high calling of motherhood.

As we come to the end of this book, I hope you've felt God speaking to you in some way or another. I have shared from my experiences, which are unique to my family and me. However, if you've gotten some new ideas or perspectives about doing life with your kids, then I am happy to have written this book. Writing this book has been a hard process for me, not because I don't enjoy writing, or it is difficult for me to put thoughts down. Rather, it has been difficult to share my personal experiences. It's also been challenging to express the methods that have worked for us as a family, because I don't want it to appear that I am telling people what to do. Just know this: this book is my response to a call from God; it's more an act of obedience to His gentle, persistent nudge rather than my desire to tell you or anyone else what to do! As you close this book, having hopefully gained some new and different insight, I wish you a good day or night of peace, hope and joy because your great God chose you to be a mother and He is helping you...yes, He is helping you every single day. As the well-known hymn goes, *"Turn your eyes upon Jesus and look full on his wonderful face..."*

APPENDIX 1

Books on Disciplining Children from a Biblical Viewpoint
You may not agree with all the principles described by each author. However, you can pray and consider a few principles shared by the authors that might work best for your family and your situation. I've found all these books helpful in various ways. Some helped me more with my disciplining approach, whereas others helped me in getting to know the heart issues of my kids better:

Campbell, Ross. *How to Really Love Your Child.* Colorado Springs, CO: David C. Cook, 2004.

Clarkson, Clay. *Heartfelt Discipline: Following God's Path of Life to the Heart of Your Child.* Monument, CO: Whole Heart Press, 2012.

Clarkson, Sally. *The Mission of Motherhood: Touching Your Child's Heart for Eternity.* Colorado Springs, CO: WaterBrook Press, 2003.

Cloud, Henry, and John Sims Townsend. *Boundaries with Kids: How Healthy Choices Grow Healthy Children.* Grand Rapids: Zondervan, 1998.

Dobson, James C. *The New Strong-willed Child.* Carol Stream, IL: Tyndall Momentum, 2014.

Durbin, Kara. *Parenting with Scripture: A Topical Guide for Teachable Moments.* Chicago, IL: Moody Press, 2012.

Eggerichs, Emerson. *Love & Respect in the Family: The Respect Parents Desire, the Love Children Need.* Nashville, TN: Thomas Nelson, 2013.

Lee, Nicky, and Sila Lee. *The Parenting Book.* London: Alpha International, 2009.

Plowman, Ginger. *Don't Make Me Count to Three!: A Mom's Look at Heart-oriented Discipline.* Wapwallopen, PA: Shepherd Press, 2003.

Tripp, Tedd. *Shepherding a Child's Heart.* Wapwallopen, PA: Shepherd Press, 1995.

APPENDIX 2

Books on Growing in Marriage

I must say that some marriage books helped me a lot in the early days of marriage, or even before I got married. I found good biblical guidance needed for living a Christ-centered marriage in these books. They've helped me, not only in area of my marriage, but also in my personal Christian growth, since I was a fairly new Christian when I got married. I've found it helpful to get new pointers about living a married life, close to God, in different seasons of my marriage. Some mentioned here are books for couples, whereas some others are addressed specifically to women.

Chapman, Gary D. *The 5 Love Languages: The Secret to Love That Lasts.* Reprint. Chicago: Northfield Pub., 2015.

Dillow, Linda, and Lorraine Pintus. *Intimate Issues: Conversations Woman to Woman: 21 Questions Christian Women Ask about Sex.* Colorado Springs, CO: WaterBrook Press, 1999.

Eggerichs, Emerson. *Love & Respect: The Love She Most Desires, the Respect He Desperately Needs.* Nashville, TN: Integrity Publishers, 2004.

Feldhahn, Shaunti. *For Women Only: What You Need to Know about the Inner Lives of Men.* Sisters, Or.: Multnomah Publishers, 2004.

George, Elizabeth. *A Wife After God's Own Heart / 12 Things That Really Matter in Your Marriage.* Eugene, OR: Harvest House Pub, 2004.

Keller, Timothy, and Kathy Keller. *The Meaning of Marriage: Facing the Complexities of Commitment with the Wisdom of God.* Reprint. Grand Rapids, IL: Penguin Books, 2013.

Smalley, Gary. *Hidden Keys of a Loving, Lasting Marriage: A Valuable Guide to Knowing, Understanding, and Loving Each Other.* Grand Rapids, MI: Zondervan Pub. House, 1993.

Smalley, Gary. *For Better or for Best: A Valuable Guide to Knowing, Understanding, and Loving Your Husband.* Grand Rapids, MI: Zondervan, 2012.

Thomas, Gary. *Sacred Marriage: What If God Designed Marriage to Make Us Holy More than to Make Us Happy?* Reprint. Grand Rapids, MI: Zondervan Pub. House, 2015.

Tripp, Paul David. *What Did You Expect?: Redeeming the Realities of Marriage.* Redesign. Wheaton, IL: Crossway Books, 2015.

NOTES

[1] Edward W. Goodrick, and John R. Kohlberger III., *The Strongest NIV Exhaustive Concordance* (Grand Rapids: Zondervan, 2004), 1466.

[2] Ross Campbell, *How to Really Love Your Child* (Colorado Springs, CO: David C. Cook, 2004), 91-92.

[3] Nicky Lee and Sila Lee, *The Parenting Book* (London: Alpha International, 2009), 175.

[4] A. H. Maslow, "The Dynamics Of Psychological Security-Insecurity," J Personality 10, no. 4 (1942): 335, doi:10.1111/j.1467-6494.1942.tb01911.x.

[5] John Bowlby, *Attachment and Loss: V. 2: Separation - Anxiety and Anger* (New York: Basic Books, 1973), 40.

[6] Patrick T. Davies and E. Mark Cummings, "Marital Conflict and Child Adjustment: An Emotional Security Hypothesis," *Psychological Bulletin* 116, no. 3 (1994), doi:10.1037/0033-2909.116.3.387.

[7] Susan Goldberg, Joan E. Grusec, and Jennifer M. Jenkins, "Confidence in Protection: Arguments for a Narrow Definition of Attachment," *Journal of Family Psychology* 13, no. 4 (1999), doi:10.1037/0893-3200.13.4.475.

[8] Patrick T. Davies and E. Mark Cummings, "Marital Conflict and Child Adjustment: An Emotional Security Hypothesis," *Psychological Bulletin* 116, no. 3 (1994), doi:10.1037/0033-2909.116.3.387.

[9] "Separation Anxiety," Psychology Today, 1991, accessed February 17, 2016, https://www.psychologytoday.com/conditions/separation-anxiety.

[10] L. Alan Sroufe, Nancy E. Fox, and Van R. Pancake, "Attachment and Dependency in Developmental Perspective," *Child Development* 54, no. 6 (December 1983), doi:10.1111/j.1467-8624.1983.tb00078.x.

[11] Patrick T. Davies and E. Mark Cummings, "Marital Conflict and Child Adjustment: An Emotional Security Hypothesis," *Psychological Bulletin* 116, no. 3 (1994), doi:10.1037/0033-2909.116.3.387.

[12] Edith Shaeffer, *What is a Family?* (Great Britain: Hodder and Stoughton, 1975), 93.

[13] Sally Clarkson, *The Mission of Motherhood* (Colorado Springs: Waterbrook, 2003). 129.

[14] Sally Clarkson, *The Mission of Motherhood* (Colorado Springs: Waterbrook, 2003). 130.

[15] Henry Cloud and John Townsend, *Boundaries with Kids: How Healthy Choices Grow Healthy Children* (United States: Zondervan, 2001), 13-23.

[16] Krystine Batcho, "Childhood Happiness: More Than Just Child's Play," Psychology Today, January 13, 2012, accessed February 18, 2016, https://www.psychologytoday.com/blog/longing-nostalgia/201201/childhood-happiness-more-just-childs-play.

[17] James F. Clapp and Catherine Cram, *Exercising Through Your Pregnancy*, 2nd ed. (Omaha, NE: Addicus Books, 2012), 1-35.

[18] Sascha Watkins, "How Many Calories a Day do I need While I'm Pregnant?", Babycentre UK, May 2013, accessed February 20, 2016, http://www.babycentre.co.uk/x568598/how-many-calories-a-day-do-i-need-while-im-pregnant.

[19] Sara Riordan, "Is It Safe to Eat Soft Cheese During Pregnancy", Babycenter, October, 2015, accessed February 20, 2016, http://www.babycenter.com/404_is-it-safe-to-eat-soft-cheese-during-pregnancy_3175.bc

[20] Xiaoping Weng, Roxana Odouli, and De-Kun Li, "Maternal Caffeine Consumption During Pregnancy and the Risk of Miscarriage: A Prospective Cohort Study," *American Journal of Obstetrics and Gynecology* 198, no. 3 (March 2008), doi:10.1016/j.ajog.2007.10.803.

[21] "Foods and Beverages to Avoid During Pregnancy", Babycenter, May, 2015, accessed February 20, 2016, http://www.babycenter.com/0_foods-and-beverages-to-avoid-during-pregnancy_10348544.bc?page=3#articlesection6

[22] "Exercise During Pregnancy", WebMD, accessed February, 21, 2016, http://www.webmd.com/baby/guide/exercise-during-pregnancy

[23] "TV Violence and Children," American Academy of Child and Adolescent Psychiatry, December 13, 2014, accessed March 30, 2016, http://www.aacap.org/AACAP/Families_and_Youth/Facts_for_Families/Facts_for_Families_Pages/Children_And_TV_Violence_13.aspx.

Printed in the United States
By Bookmasters